# KANSAS
# STORMS

## DEDICATION

This book is dedicated to the Real Heroes – The 20 Kansans who lost their lives, the survivors, and the thousands of emergency workers and volunteers who rushed to help.

A portion of the proceeds of this book will be donated to the Mennonite Disaster Service to help them continue their vital work.

# KANSAS STORMS

## DESTRUCTION, TRAGEDY & RECOVERY • 1991

Diane Silver
Editor

Hearth Publishing
A Division of Multi Business Press
Hillsboro, Kansas

# Acknowledgements

Many people have contributed their enthusiasm, time and hard work to this project. Without their efforts, this book would never have become a reality.

The National Weather Service contributed time, expertise, and open access to its many detailed reports. Fred Ostby, director of the National Severe Storms Forecast Center, and Jim Henderson, deputy director of the center, patiently taught me the reality behind the myths about tornadoes and the weather warning system. Bill Fortune of the Weather Service office in Topeka spent hours helping me unsnarl the confusion of the 1991 storm season and then patiently reviewed the manuscript for scientific accuracy. Jon Davies, Pratt businessman and meteorologist, gave me the initial help I needed to start researching the book.

Dillions Stores gave vital support early in the project.

Eight journalists provided their expertise and more. Janet Majure, Roberta Birk, Carol Duerksen, Lesia Curry, Richard Hensley, Connie White, Susan Kraus, and Larry Peirce tracked down leads, snapped photos and helped out at receptions along with preparing their chapters. Thanks also to Janet for providing her expertise in copy editing. Many thanks to Carol for providing the voice of experience from Hearth's 1990 storms book. Tony Peterson did a marvelous job of pulling together hundreds of pages of reports to produce the table on the cost of the 1991 storm season.

Thanks to all the good folks at Hearth Publishing who organized receptions, provided refreshments and welcomed a new editor with warmth and wit. Judy Boschmann and Joel Klaassen were vital helps. The vision of Stan Thiessen, president of Hearth, sparked and sustained this project. Stan also very ably took over the huge job of collecting the photographs. Stan and Judy picked the photos and planned the photo essays. Stan even allowed himself to be pulled into researching one of the chapters. Hearty thanks also to Dave Ranney for connecting me with Hearth.

My heartfelt thanks to my family for putting up with my long absences, my long nights at the computer and my endless stories about tornadoes.

Finally, the warmest thank you goes to the hundreds of Kansans who shared their time, stories and photographs. Their openness and willingness to help was truly remarkable.

– Diane Silver, Editor

CREDITS:

Front Cover: Tornado strikes electrical transformer 1 mile north and 1/2 east of Arkansas City. Photo by Joel Day.

Back Cover: Vicki Stien and Vonda Mock embrace after seeing destruction at Cox Farm. Photo by Keith Lathrom.

Design: Concept by Denise Siemens. Technical Design by D. Andrew West. Desktop Implementation by Nancy Unruh.

FIRST EDITION: Copyright ©1991 by Multi Business Press
ISBN: 0-9627947-3-2
Library of Congress Catalog Number 91-75973

# Table of Contents

# Introduction

# The Fury of Kansas Weather

I first met the fury of Kansas weather on a hot, muggy Tuesday afternoon at 19th and Vermont streets in Lawrence while driving my 5-year-old son to a babysitter. When we had started out a few minutes before, the lawns and trees had been green, the first spring flowers pink and purple. But at 4:40 p.m. the sky, in fact the whole world around us, turned gray as torrents of rain rocked my tiny Escort wagon. Then the sound started.

First, a delicate ping on the car's metal roof, then another ping, then an avalanche. It sounded as if giants were hurtling chunks of steel at us from all sides, hard balls at 90 miles an hour. Seated behind me in a child restraint seat, my son Tony started to cry. I didn't dare look back because I was busy trying to see out of a windshield that had been turned opaque by curtains of rain and dirty white rocks bouncing off the hood in front of me. I found a road, turned slowly, guessed at the curb and eased the car over to it.

I shut off the car and turned to Tony. His eyes were squeezed shut, his fingers jammed in his ears and he was crying, softly I thought. Climb into the front seat, I yelled. We were surrounded by sound — wham, wham, whamming. What I thought was his quiet crying must have been very loud because I could barely hear myself shout. Tony wiggled out of his car seat, quickly clambered over to the front and crawled into my lap. I hugged him and tried to make him turn his face to my chest because it seemed so suddenly and achingly clear that the car I had always loved for its wide, open view was full of windows that could break any second.

Then it was over.

Bing.

Bing.

Silence.

I looked up but couldn't see a thing. The windows were thickly fogged. The windshield was half buried in hailstones, piled on the black line of the windshield wiper. I took a deep breath. Tony wiped his cheeks with the back of his hand. I leaned forward and pulled on the door handle. The door fell open.

Freezing air, 20 degrees cooler than minutes before, gushed in. We peered out into a landscape of stones, snow drifts of them, piled up white against the curbs and carpeting the pavement. Tony slid off my lap onto the passenger seat and I stepped out into a changed world. Even the ground was changed, suddenly slippery with rolling balls of ice.

I had grown up in Michigan, supposedly a Midwestern native hardened to the roughness of

Midwestern weather. I had lived in Kansas for almost six years, but I had never experienced anything like this. In 10 minutes, the environment had been transformed. The stones buried flowers and lawns so that all color appeared to have been taken from the world. I even felt different. Something in me was trembling as I stepped out of that car. It was something that had not been trembling before.

Yet I had gotten only a small taste of the fury of Kansas weather. The hailstorm that inflicted more than $22 million damage in Lawrence on March 26 was nothing, absolutely nothing, compared to the storms thousands of other people endured during the disastrous Kansas storm season of 1991.

The most horrible day of all was April 26. An estimated 20 tornadoes swept through the state, including a funnel that traveled through Sedgwick and Butler counties. That tornado cut through Haysville, south Wichita, McConnell Air Force Base and Andover before skipping north to terrorize motorists on the Kansas Turnpike.

Along its route, houses and businesses were smashed, cars and trucks were tossed through the air. By the time the tornado finally dissipated north of El Dorado, 17 people were dead, hundreds were injured, and almost 2,000 homes were damaged or destroyed. Most of the deaths occurred in a mobile home park in Andover.

Lost in the news coverage of that tornado — particularly the events in Andover — were other tragedies of April 26. Tornadoes in nearby Cowley and Elk counties killed two people. Twisters swept through Jefferson and Atchison counties, smashing farms and finally destroying homes in the small town of Nortonville.

Kansans also had to deal with other onslaughts in 1991. On March 26, for instance, the same day as the Lawrence hailstorm, a series of tornadoes destroyed homes in Pratt and Reno counties in south-central Kansas.

At times in 1991, it seemed as if nothing would remain untouched by the weather. A University of Kansas landmark, Hoch Auditorium, was struck by lightning, and the resulting fire gutted the building.

In only the first six months of 1991, 115 tornadoes thundered through Kansas, according to the National Weather Service.

The horror of the 1991 storm season was intensified by the fact that the year before a series of tornadoes destroyed much of Hesston, smashed through houses in Marion and McPherson counties, hit suburbs of Topeka and destroyed homes in Emporia. Two people died in those storms. In all, 88 tornadoes ground through Kansas in 1990. Floods and high winds from thunderstorms also damaged towns throughout the state.

Meteorologists explain that the fury of the weather is fueled by an accident of geography. The state's location makes it the meeting place for opposites. Wherever opposites meet in the atmosphere, storms are born.

In the case of Kansas and the rest of the central Plains, the opposites consist of the warm, moist air mass that blows north every spring from the Gulf of Mexico and the dry, cold air that streams south from Canada and the Arctic. To the west of Kansas, the towering wall of the Rocky Mountains funnels the air masses down to the Plains.

These conditions, along with others, guarantee that the central Plains will be the birthplace of severe thunderstorms. Every one of those storms has the potential to spawn tornadoes, damaging hail, flood-creating downpours and dangerous lightning.

All of this puts Kansas in the middle of what has been dubbed "Tornado Alley," a diagonal swath of real estate that includes northern Texas, Oklahoma, Kansas and parts of Nebraska and Missouri. Although tornadoes occur in almost every state and many countries, Tornado Alley has more tornadoes than anyplace else on the globe.

But meteorological explanations do not tell the whole story of Kansas' violent weather. Discussions of air masses cannot convey the horror, exhilaration, anger, irritation, faith, exhaustion, humor and sheer guts of the people who lived through the 1991 Kansas storm season. Through words and photographs, this book will attempt to do that. In a small way, this book will also attempt to honor the lives of the Kansans who died in the storms.

However, this book does have an unfortunate limitation. It is far too short to include every story that should be mentioned. The lives of thousands of Kansans were changed by these storms, yet we only have space to show the experiences of a few people.

The information for this book was compiled by a staff of eight professional journalists. Most of the photographs came from amateurs. Many were snapping frames of funnels as they hurried for shelter. Other amateurs documented the agony and frustrations of their struggles to rebuild their lives.

Throughout all of their work is one theme — a common reality that has helped me understand what was trembling inside when I stepped out of my car into the aftermath of the Lawrence hailstorm.

In an age when we humans tend to believe that our technology has made us supreme upon the Earth, these storms are teaching us an important lesson. Different people talk about the lesson in different ways. Many Kansans quoted in the book talk about the storms as evidence of God's power upon the Earth. Other Kansans talk about nature's power. For me, the best example of the meaning of the storms came at McConnell Air Force Base.

Shortly before the tornado ground through the base, U.S. forces in the Mideast proved the power and the efficiency of a whole new generation of hardware by smashing the Iraqi military. But on April 26, far from the guns of the Mideast, the huge tornado churned toward a line of the Pentagon's most powerful jets that were parked at McConnell. Two of the planes were even loaded with nuclear warheads, according to newspaper reports.

With winds swirling at speeds ranging from 113 to 157 miles per hour, the tornado could have picked up the bombers and tossed them like toys.

The tornado passed within 2,000 yards of planes. No gun on Earth, no bomb, no attack plane could have stopped the funnel if it had veered toward the planes. All the men and women of McConnell could do was hide and pray.

— Diane Silver,
Lawrence, Kansas

**Left: This pile of hailstones was collected one mile east of Lawrence on Kansas Highway 10. Photo by David Babb.**

**Fog forms over piles of hailstones and leaves torn off trees cover part of a road west of Lawrence. Photo by Jeff Manion.**

# March 26

The first serious damage of the 1991 storm season occurred on March 26. Thunderstorms rolling across the state produced tornadoes, severe hail and heavy winds. The weather service recorded reports of almost a dozen tornadoes on March 26. More than 80 locations reported hail.

Tornadoes dropped down on Pratt and Reno counties, causing extensive damage. The town of Abbyville and the Hutchinson suburb of Willowbrook were particularly hard hit. Tornado strikes were also reported in Cowley and Allen counties.

Damaging hail fell many places throughout the state. Hail inflicted the greatest damage on Lawrence and the University of Kansas.

Before the day was over, straight winds gusting to over 80 miles per hour would sweep across much of Kansas, causing a total of $1.5 million damage.

*"It was a sunny, beautiful day with a forecast for two or three more just like it."*
–Glenn Sohl

# Lawrence

The day started sunny and warm. The temperature reached a record high of 85. On the hill overlooking Lawrence, students and faculty at the University of Kansas were working toward the end of the school year less than two months away. Down the hill near the center of town, Glenn Sohl wondered if this was the right time to continue remodeling work on his restaurant, Cornucopia. In the end, the weather made him decide that this was the perfect day to work on the next step — tearing out the building's front wall.

"It was a sunny, beautiful day with a forecast for two or three more just like it," Sohl says.

By the time the National Weather Service issued a severe thunderstorm warning at 4:30 p.m., black,

turbulent clouds had already begun to roll in. Across town, people went to their windows, stepped out on porches to look at the sky. In minutes, the temperature plummeted 20 degrees. Sudden gusts of cool wind rattled windows and an intense rain fell.

Nancy Ness, an architectural artist, had just arrived home from a meeting with clients to join her husband, John, and their two teen-age sons in her ranch house in south central Lawrence. All four of them stood in front of the plate glass window in the living room and watched the sky.

"The sky was threatening, and I'd been through tornadoes before, so I have a real respect for that kind of sky," she says.

Wind and rain shook the trees. Then the hail fell. It

A mound of hail is piled up in the median of Kansas Highway 10 one mile east of Lawrence. Rain melted some of the hailstones and washed the rest into low drifts. Photo by David Babb.

started small. Balls the size of marbles tumbled out of the sky, then golf-ball sized hail and larger. It banged against the roof and bounced off the sidewalks.

"I grabbed my husband and kids and started pushing them to the basement," Ness says. "Seconds later, the entire window blew in."

As they waited in the basement, they felt the house rock. All the windows on the west side blew out. Looking out through basement windows they watched pieces of roof fly through the yard.

"We were sure it was a tornado," Ness says.

At the Robinson Center on the KU campus, graduate student Anita Ground, who was five months pregnant, had just finished playing racquetball with a friend. As they left the gym, they met a deluge of pounding rain and a wide expanse of sidewalk between them and their car, which was parked on the other side of a group of tennis courts. The two decided to run for the car. Ground handed her car keys to her friend. They dashed out into the rain.

"By the corner of the first court, the small hail had started," Ground says. "By the end of that court, it was like golf balls."

The hail came down so hard they could not see even a few feet ahead. Her friend became disoriented and turned back. Pelted by hailstones, Ground kept running. She reached the car, but realized that she was stranded outside its locked doors. The keys had gone with her friend. The sound of the hail drumming on everything was overwhelming Ground says.

"I couldn't hear anything else," she says. Ground was scared to death. Before graduate school, she had worked as a nurse in delivery rooms. She knew the seriousness of injuries during pregnancy.

"I felt very protective and frightened, for myself and my baby," she says. She felt she had to make split second decisions while also sensing that the world was in slow motion.

"I had trouble believing it was real, yet I was soaked and getting pounded," she says.

Ground realized she had to find shelter somewhere in the parking lot, and do it quickly. She decided to crawl under a nearby pick-up truck.

Before Ground could get under the truck, she saw a car with its headlights on. Ground ran to the car, and the driver opened the door to let her in. Around them, hailstones bounced off the cement as if they were small rubber balls.

Across campus at the School of Journalism, Associate Professor Ted Frederickson was writing at his office computer when he heard a tinkling sound mixed in with the drumming of the hail on his office window sills.

"I ran into the classroom across the hall, and windows were breaking," Frederickson says. "The tables were covered with hail that had blown in and bits of broken glass."

At a mobile home park on the south end of town, manager Edie Seales unlocked the storm shelter so residents could take cover. But the hail came down so hard and fast that people were too frightened to run to the shelter door. Several people drove almost to the door and then huddled in their cars, Seales says. A dash of even a few feet was too dangerous.

"The hail would have knocked a person out cold," Seales says.

**Rain pushed these hailstones into a drift on West 31st Street. Photo by Allen R. Bartels.**

At the Cornucopia Restaurant, Sohl and his work crew had succeeded in tearing down part of the wall by the time the rain started. Within minutes, hail pelted the inside of the building and ricocheted off a wall 18 feet inside. Sohl and his crew moved back to take shelter inside the building. At the time, the storm seemed almost funny. There was nothing else the crew could do but laugh at their predicament

"We picked up 2 X 4's and had batting practice with the hail," he says. "It was certainly big enough."

A few blocks from downtown, Leni Salkind and her family were waiting out the storm in her home in Old West Lawrence, an historic neighborhood of stately homes.

"It was like a barrage of gunfire, that loud and scary," Salkind says. "We could see chunks of ice falling from the sky."

The hail shredded the screens in their windows. Salkind's neighbors later reported seeing hail bouncing 30 feet into the air after hitting Salkind's roof.

Across town at Central Junior High, students were finishing a play rehearsal. As the school loudspeaker warned students and teachers to take cover, play director Chuck Holley kept his students away from the windows. Hail careened in through the open windows and knocked against the metal lockers.

At Laird Noller Motors, employees frantically tried to drive the new cars to safety, but they could save only a few of the 300 vehicles on the lot.

"We couldn't even see across the street," said Kim Hodges, a Laird Noller employee. "It was a solid wall of hail."

In 10 minutes, the hail stopped, even the rain stopped. When Nancy Ness and her family emerged from the basement, the hail was so deep they had to push it away from the doors with a shovel. Everywhere were piles of white hailstones, ranging in size from walnuts to twice as big as golf balls. The hollow-core side door on their house was in strips and pieces. The wooden garage door was gouged and strips of wood had splintered.

"Every leaf was gone from the tree," Ness says. "We couldn't find a flower. The roof was punched with holes clear through a new roof and down to the bottom layer."

Hailstones mixed with shards of glass from the broken windows lined the inside walls of the house.

But Ness wasn't upset. She stepped into her front yard and danced. It was a dance of sheer relief, she says.

"The house was still standing. We were still here, and even our pets were still alive."

In the parking lot of the Robinson Center, Anita Ground discovered that she was covered with bruises, but she was not seriously injured. Ground says she found herself over and over again thanking the driver who had given her shelter.

In the Gaslight Village mobile home park, residents comforted two 9-year-old children who had been caught outside in the hail while running to the park storm shelter. The children's heads were covered with lumps. They had bruises and scratches. Throughout the mobile home park, roofs were pitted and siding was dented. Windows throughout the area were broken. Cars were deeply dented.

*"It was like a barrage of gunfire, that loud and scary. We could see chunks of ice falling from the sky."*

–Leni Salkind

Rain mixes with hail on West 31st Street. Notice the hail piled onto the deck and drifted against the siding. Photo by Allen R. Bartels.

In the first few moments after the storm passed, the hail was piled so deep that it made walking treacherous, says manager Seales.

"It was like walking on ice balls to try and get across the lawn," she says.

At the Cornucopia Restaurant, owner Sohl discovered that the storm had taken a toll. The restaurant's neon signs had been destroyed and the roof damaged, he says.

In Old West Lawrence, the Salkind house had sustained damage, but the family was safe.

In minutes, more than $22 million in damage had occurred. Later local residents would file more than 9,500 insurance claims, but no one was seriously injured.

One person was cut by the hail and received stitches at Lawrence Memorial Hospital's emergency room. Many people called asking how to get broken glass out of their hair, says Judith McFadden, the hospital's director of community relations.

At the university, 200 windows broke. About 20 trees were severely damaged or destroyed. Roofs were damaged. Virtually every vehicle on campus had a cracked or shattered window or a pitted hood.

In the city, public school officials counted about 50 broken skylights along with broken windows and damaged roofs and vehicles.

At the car dealerships on the edge of town hundreds of new and used cars had been damaged. Dented sides and shattered windows reduced the values of each car by thousands of dollars.

Despite the damage, Lawrence had been lucky. Most of the damage was covered by insurance. Because the hail had been concentrated in town, few farmers reported crop damage. For some car owners, the insurance money they received for their dented vehicles was an unexpected windfall. Despite the dents, the cars still ran. Some owners pocketed their insurance money, using it to take impromptu vacations or to pay off their bills. Meanwhile, business boomed for auto body shops and roofing companies.

For people like Ground, the only lasting reminder of the hailstorm was a vivid memory. Ground recovered fully from her experience. On July 28, she delivered a healthy boy and named him Eric.

Months later the only real sign of the storm would be the huge hailstones that had been stashed in freezers and the pitted cars.

The rest of Kansas would not be so fortunate. Δ

Monty Davis snapped this photo of the tornado before taking cover in Fairfield High School. The funnel passed within 1/2 mile of the school.

Jeremy Lanning,11, runs out of the ruins of his home minutes after the tornado struck. Photographer Don Shreve had just arrived when Lanning emerged. "He just started screaming. "Shreve says. "I fired four frames, then ran up and asked him if anyone was hurt. . . I put my arm around him and tried to calm him down."

# A Good News, Bad News Day

Brothers Jim and John Ellena had a guardian angel watching over them on the day of the Lawrence hail storm. Insurance Agent Doug Zey of Overland Park wasn't so lucky.

The day started as a good one for Zey. The agent for Federated Insurance racked up the biggest commercial sale of his eight-month insurance career when he signed the Ellenas to change the coverage of their Lawrence car dealerships to his company. The change increased their coverage from about 70 percent of damages to 100 percent of damage. Negotiating the deal had taken weeks.

Zey would get a large commission from the sale. His company would get a big chunk of money from the premiums the car dealers would pay.

Smiling broadly, Zey loaded the contracts into his briefcase, got into his car and headed out of town. "It was the happiest 15 minutes of my life," Zey says.

Just as Zey reached the city limits, the hail fell. The insurance agent pulled off the road and watched as the hail piled up 3 inches deep around his car.

At first the situation was frightening for the car dealers. "I was scared to death," Jim Ellena says. "While it was hailing, it felt like a disaster. I had no idea whether the business could survive, or if I'd be bankrupt after 23 years. There was no way of predicting the outcome."

On the edge of town, Zey turned around his car. He headed back to the dealership. The agent looked over the dented hoods and roofs, peered at the shattered windshields and the damage to the buildings and "looked like he was going to cry," Ellena says.

After a while, Zey pulled himself together and called his boss. Zey told his boss, "I have good news and bad news."

The new policy paid the car dealership about $50,000 more than they would have received under their old policy, Jim Ellena says. Δ

*"It was the happiest 15 minutes of my life."*

–Doug Zey

# Pratt & Reno Counties

On Tuesday, March 26, four tornadoes dropped out of a thunderstorm onto Pratt and Reno counties. In their path lay open countryside, farmhouses, the modest houses of Abbyville and the stately homes of Willowbrook. Originally the country estate of Emerson Carey, the founder of the Carey Salt Co., Willowbrook was designed in the early 1920s. The tree-shaded homes overlook a golf course and are bordered by a brook on two sides.

At 5:45 p.m., the first tornado touched down near

Right: This photo was taken on the morning after the tornado demolished Jim and Juna Keevers' home. Photo by Jim Keever Jr.

Before the tornado, Jim and Juna Keever's home was tidy and secure. In June 1990, they did extensive remodeling. Photo by Jim Keever Jr.

*"There was a peculiar odor in the air, indescribable."*

–Don Shreve

Preston. The funnel came down about 1 mile from the home where Bob and Donna Schlenz have lived for 26 years near Preston. There was no warning as the twister approached their mobile home, parked near an old farmhouse and a stand of cedar trees. With no time to take cover in their storm cellar, the couple dropped to the floor in a hallway.

"Bob said he didn't have time to be scared," Donna says. "Well, I had time to be scared. It just roared."

The tornado struck and then rumbled away from their house, skipping through the countryside, damaging houses, irrigation sprinklers and farm machinery before dissipating four miles north of Preston. A weak tornado, the funnel's winds were estimated to be swirling at 75 miles per hour.

Northeast of the Schlenzes' between the towns of Preston and Turon, the thunderstorm threw down another funnel. Much stronger than the first, this tornado's winds reached speeds of 175 miles per hour.

The funnel swirled to the northeast, damaging outbuildings at Lois Gabriel's farm, sucking up trees and grain bins from Briant and Annie Hacking's farm. The funnel cut a path parallel to Kansas Highway 61, passing within one-half mile of Fairfield High School. Because of the time, school was not in session. The twister was about 300 yards wide. It headed north to Abbyville.

Hutchinson News photographer Don Shreve and other journalists in the paper's newsroom were monitoring the progress of the tornadoes on police scanners. Although other photographers had already been sent to cover the storm, Shreve soon received permission from his boss to go after the story. Shreve

hurried to his car and headed toward the most recent report of a sighting.

Before he was even close, Shreve could see the tornado. Shreve caught up with the tornado southwest of Abbyville in the country. Zigzagging down one dirt road after another, Shreve tracked the funnel for seven miles. He was a half a mile behind the tornado. The funnel was short, wide, fat. It was dark gray and shrouded in rain.

"There was a peculiar odor in the air, indescribable" Shreve says.

Just northeast of Shreve, Sharon and Allan Moore had been working in the garden on their farm that afternoon. They came inside and soon heard the tornado warning on television. They heard sirens from emergency vehicles and headed to the storm cellar.

At the top of the steps, Allan pulled the cellar door shut. Almost immediately, the wind blew the door away. They ran down the steps and sat in the northwest corner.

"I was very scared, but we heard nothing except tin banging around," Sharon says.

By 6:41 p.m., the tornado had weakened to the point where its winds were rotating at 60 to 75 miles per hour. But the storm still had enough power to overturn the truck John Snyder of Abbyville was driving. Snyder was pinned inside.

Four minutes later and nine miles southwest of Hutchinson, the thunderstorm produced the largest tornado it was to spawn that day. Winds inside the funnel were estimated at speeds as high as 260 miles per hour.

Just west of Hutchinson, Ron Heironimus was

working in his yard. His wife Carol and their children, Tracy 17, and Rob, 29, and Tracy's friend Ryan Hale were getting ready to attend a concert at Nickerson High School. The radio provided reports of numerous tornado sightings, but the group heard no sirens. Their first warning came when Ron rushed into the house. "It's coming our way," Ron said.

The five ran into an inside hallway. Seconds later the tornado enveloped the house, shaking and lifting it from its foundation. Carol grabbed her daughter's hand and held on tight. She felt her daughter's hand slipping from her grasp and then all five people were sucked into the air. The house blew apart.

At the same moment, oral surgeon Howard Thompson was driving as fast as he could toward Willowbrook. He knew that his wife Charlotte was home. She uses a wheelchair, and he was terrified that she would not be able to make it to the basement.

The sky was black and it was raining hard. As he neared Willowbrook, Thompson counted three tornadoes surging toward the 36 stately, tree-shaded homes that made up Willowbrook. But he had no time to gawk. Thompson sped down the road. He made it home before any of the twisters hit.

Running into the house, Thompson found Charlotte sitting in her wheelchair in the entryway. He pushed her down a hallway and onto the electric wheelchair lift that runs beside the stairs. Thompson pushed the button, and the lift started to descend, Thompson walked down the stairs beside the lift. The power went off. The lift stopped. Moments later, the power came back on and the lift started down again, then the power flicked off

and came on. After what seemed an eternity, the lift reached the basement floor. Within seconds, the tornado struck. Glass shattered above them. The house shuddered.

Nearby, H.J. "Jake" Carey, Jr., the grandson of Willowbrook's founder was home alone. His wife was visiting relatives in Baltimore. He had just brought home chicken and cole slaw when he turned on the television to check on the weather. He heard the tornado warnings, picked up a radio and flashlight, and went to the basement. Carey heard a whoosh and saw dust in the air. The pressure in his ears changed. Ceiling tiles fell to the floor. The lights went out.

The tornado ground toward Nickerson. It missed the town by six miles before dissipating.

At 7:20 p.m., a fourth tornado touched down one mile southwest of Inman. It hopscotched through the fields, damaging farms before disappearing back into the clouds two miles northeast of Inman.

As the last tornado disappeared, people began to emerge from their hiding places.

Donna and Bob Schlenz survived a wild ride in their mobile home without even an injury. But when they looked around their home, they saw that the roof was gone. Cedar limbs were sticking through the walls. All but one window had broken, even though curtains still neatly framed each shattered window. Their front door had vanished. Despite the damage, 18 head of cattle, a dog, a cat and two guinea pigs survived the storm.

Hutchinson News photographer Don Shreve lost track of the tornado when he stopped to move tree

*" It's coming our way!"*

–Ron Heironimus

The tornado tore the center out of Peggy and Jake Carey's house in Willowbrook.

Right: A volunteer helping with the cleanup in Willowbrook takes a break. Photo by Larry Swank.

*"He made it up here with two flat front tires."*

–Sharon Moore

limbs out of the road. Shreve got back into his car and drove to survey the damage.

Shreve discovered a damaged farm. Rubble was heaped where there had once been a house. Debris filled the yard. Shreve stopped to photograph the scene. A boy came screaming up from steps leading underground. Shreve quickly shot four frames and then ran to try to comfort the boy.

The boy, Jeremy Lanning, 11, was frantic to find his dog Duchess. When Jeremy emerged from the basement, he immediately saw that the grain bin where the dog had been chained had vanished. Jeremy ignored Shreve and ran searching for Duchess. He later found the dog, uninjured, under the limbs of a downed tree.

Jeremy and his uncle, Mike Lanning, had ridden out the storm together in the basement.

In the first moments after the tornado, Sharon and Allan Moore felt relief. They were safe. They climbed to the top of the basement stairs: Their two-story farmhouse was still standing.

But walking through the house, the Moores discovered a bizarre mixture of mud and straw coating everything. The mixture was sticking through empty windows, plastered against inside walls, eerily patterning floors and furniture. Looking out the broken windows, Sharon noticed that only a few of the dozens of huge, round bales of hay that had been sitting in the field across the road were still there. Looking at their house more carefully, the Moores discovered that the tornado must have twisted the entire structure. Doors stuck out in odd positions.

Outside their home, stood a vast rubble heap composed of straw, farm machinery and bits of metal that had once been part of the walls of sheds.

After the storm, their son Brian tried to reach his parents, but he was stopped by a police roadblock. From the barricade, Brian could see that his parent's home had been damaged. Brian backed his car away from the roadblock, drove up on a railroad embankment and sped over the tracks, flying into the air like Evil Knievel.

"He made it up here with two flat front tires," Sharon says.

At the intersection of Kansas Highway 14 and Fourth Avenue west of Hutchinson, truck driver John Snyder was pinned inside his rig for over an hour after the tornado turned over his truck. When he was finally freed, doctors discovered that Snyder had suffered two broken bones in his left leg.

Just west of Hutchinson, Ron and Carol Heironimus and their family had been tossed 70 feet from their house. They were battered, bruised and cut. A gray, pasty film covered them.

Carol Heironimus came to her senses sprawled in mud. She looked around and saw that everyone had been thrown to the southwest of the house except her daughter Tracy. She was lying motionless to the east.

Carol and Tracy's friend, Ryan Hale, walked through the debris-strewn field to Tracy while Ron hobbled to the still form of his son, Rob.

Rob did not appear to be breathing as he lay in a field. He was covered with debris. For one long, terrible moment, his father thought his son was dead. Frantically, Ron screamed his son's name and dropped to the ground to shake the motionless body. Rob gasped for

air. A friend arrived, and helped Ron dig his son out. Father and son hurried to Tracy.

Her face was covered in blood, but she was awake. She could not get to her feet. The family and Hale huddled around her. The five were still in the field when an ambulance arrived 10 minutes later.

Later, the family learned that Tracy had suffered a broken nose, facial cuts and a broken vertebra. She was not paralyzed. Ron had suffered a broken knee.

In Willowbrook, Howard and Charlotte Thompson emerged from the basement and found that the tornado had torn the roof off their home and made a shambles of the interior. The couple, though, was safe.

When Jake Carey came upstairs, it was still dark and raining. A hole gaped in the middle section of the roof covering his house. Rain was pouring in. The chimney lay in the living room. Outside, a roofed terrace had been demolished. Its metal latticework had been flung aside. Debris surrounded the house. Looking around, Carey saw that Willowbrook's trees had been sheared as if by some monstrous barber. Carey was not injured.

It had been a harrowing day in Pratt and Reno counties. People had been injured and terrified. Seven of the 36 homes of Willowbrook had been leveled and 20 had been damaged. In the rest of Reno County, alone, 16 other homes had been destroyed. The cost of the damage would reach far into the millions. Δ

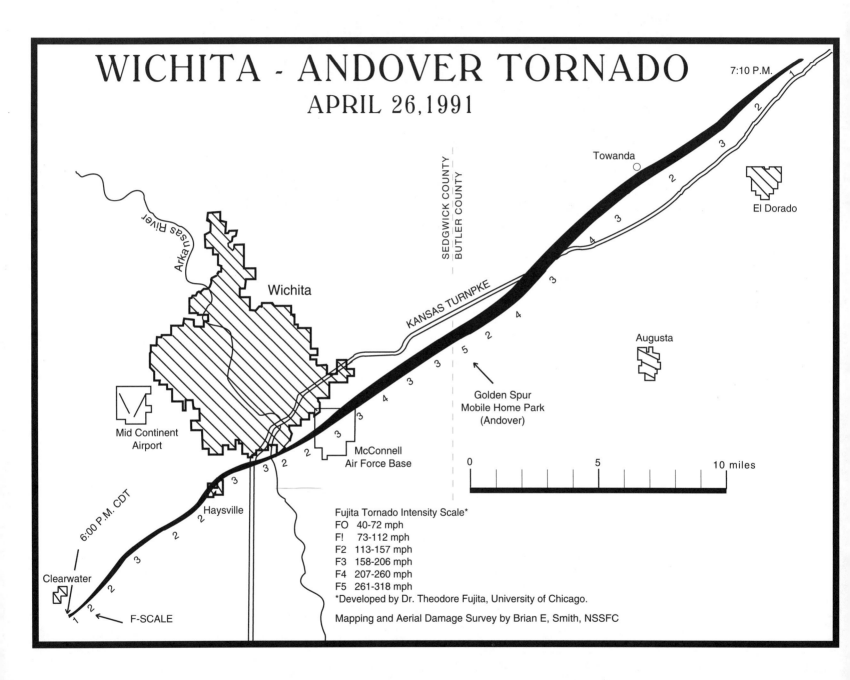

# WICHITA - ANDOVER TORNADO
## APRIL 26, 1991

7:10 P.M.

Towanda

El Dorado

SEDGWICK COUNTY
BUTLER COUNTY

Arkansas River

Wichita

KANSAS TURNPKE

Augusta

Mid Continent
Airport

Golden Spur
Mobile Home Park
(Andover)

McConnell
Air Force Base

6:00 P.M. CDT

Haysville

Clearwater

F-SCALE

0      5      10 miles

Fujita Tornado Intensity Scale*
FO   40-72 mph
F!    73-112 mph
F2   113-157 mph
F3   158-206 mph
F4   207-260 mph
F5   261-318 mph
*Developed by Dr. Theodore Fujita, University of Chicago.

Mapping and Aerial Damage Survey by Brian E, Smith, NSSFC

One of the first photos of the storm that devestated Sedgwick and Bulter counties shows it threatening north-central Haysville. A wide, dark funnel is visible in the background. Smaller white funnels are in the foreground. Photo by Don Blecha.

# April 26

On April 26 severe thunderstorms swept over the Plains, producing 56 tornadoes from Texas to Nebraska. In Kansas as many as 20 funnels were reported on the ground. More than 110 locations reported large hail.

The most destructive tornado of the day was one of a family of four tornadoes created by a huge thunderstorm that developed over north-central Oklahoma and moved northeast over south-central Kansas, according to the Weather Service.

The funnel first dropped out of the sky at 5:57 p.m. approximately 2 miles east of Clearwater in Sedgwick County. Moving to the northeast, the tornado reached Haysville by 6:16 p.m.. At this point, winds inside the funnel were swirling at speeds as high as 206 miles per hour. The tornado had already reached the F2 and F3 rating to rank as a "significant tornado" and then a "severe tornado" on the Fujita Tornado Scale.

*"Automobile-size missles fly through the air ... trees debarked; incredible phenomena will occur."*

–Journal of Atmosphere Science

At 6:23 p.m., the tornado tracked through McConnell Air Force Base near Wichita. The funnel's path was between 500 and 600 feet wide. By the time the tornado crossed Andover Road and began entering the Golden Spur Mobile Home Park in Andover at 6:40 p.m., the storm had intensified to the F5 level — the level of an "incredible tornado", capable of lifting frame houses off their foundations and carrying them through the air until they disintegrate.

"Automobile-size missles fly through the air ... trees debarked; incredible phenomena will occur," according to an article in the 1981 Journal of Atmospheric Science.

At this point, the funnel contained winds swirling at speeds up to 318 miles per hour. The tornado's path was 2,000 feet wide.

As the tornado sped out of Andover and traveled along the Kansas Turnpike, the funnel's force weakened. The tornado dissipated 10 miles northeast of Wichita near the town of El Dorado at about 7 p.m. The tornado had traveled 46 miles in slightly more than one hour.

In all, four people died in the neighborhoods of south Wichita. Another 11 people were killed in the mobile home park in Andover. Two people died on the road near the mobile home park. Hundreds of people were injured. Many of the injuries were severe. A total of 1,728 homes were destroyed or damaged, including the almost total destruction of nearly every wall, floor, ceiling and piece of furniture that had been a part of the 241 homes of the Golden Spur Mobile Home Park in Andover. In that town alone, an estimated 855 people were made homeless by the storm.

Even after the killer tornado had dissipated, the terror

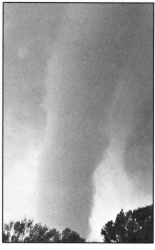

The tornado bears down on the Cox Produce Farm and market in Wichita. As the tornado approached, 19 people were working at the family-owned business to prepare it to open its doors the next day for the 1991 season. Photos by Keith Lathrom.

of the day continued. Tornadoes dipped to the ground in Cowley and Elk counties. Two people died. At 9 that night, another tornado smashed through the countryside in Jefferson County in northeastern Kansas. At 9:30 p.m. yet another twister destroyed homes in the small town of Nortonville. Δ

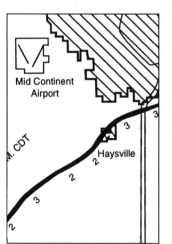

Numbers indicate strength on the Fujita scale.

# The Big One: Haysville & South Wichita

The day had all the ingredients for disaster. Strong winds from the south were pumping a layer of moist warm air up from the Gulf of Mexico. About 10,000 feet above that, strong westerly winds were pushing dry cold air from the Rocky Mountains. Above it all, the jet stream was blowing extremely strongly, reaching speeds of more than 110 knots, about 126 miles per hour. The juxtaposition of these factors was creating a strong updraft and turbulence that would spawn a huge supercell thunderstorm.

"It was an explosive day," says Dick Elder, meteorologist in charge of the National Weather Service office in Wichita.

Meteorologists throughout the region were worried. At 4 a.m. on the 26th, the National Severe Storms Forecast Center in Kansas City issued an unusual alert, warning that most of the eastern half of Kansas would be in a "high-risk" area for severe weather. At 4:50 a.m., the Weather Service office in Topeka issued its own special weather statement. Extra staff was called in to work at the Wichita weather service office and the weather station at McConnell Air Force Base.

At 12:10 p.m. the severe storm center issued a tornado watch. Effective until 8 p.m., the watch warned that conditions were ripe for damaging tornadoes in the region.

At 4:36 p.m., the Weather Service office in Wichita declared a severe thunderstorm warning.

Fifty minutes later, the Wichita office received the first report of a tornado in the area. The twister touched down briefly near the city of Anthony in Harper County.

In the Wichita office, forecasters peered intently at radar screens, searching for any clue of a tornado. But as the storms came closer to the city, the forecasters became more and more frustrated. The radar system they were using was outdated and scheduled to be replaced. It could not give a clear picture of tornado activity near the city.

"We were relying very heavily on what our spotters were telling us," Elder says.

In the Timber Lane Addition of Haysville just south of Wichita, Donna Tobler was finishing the week at the day care center she runs in her home. Only one of her eight pupils remained, and the boy's mother was due to pick him up in 20 minutes. Donna's own children, Dustin, 12, and Melanie, 8, were playing. Her husband, Tony, had come home from his job as a shipping and receiving supervisor for an industrial supplies company about 5:30

Left: Four months after the tornado struck, Wichita Tool Co. on South Seneca Street is a pile of rubble. Photo by Trish Birk.

This $130,000 combine was one of three damaged by the tornado on Jack and Chelsea McCreery's place near Clearwater. The couple was preparing to head south to harvest wheat when the tornado struck. Photo by Colleen Heitman.

p.m. Tony went to the garage to do some work and poured himself a glass of water. He set it down on the work bench where he left it when he went into the house to shower. The couple planned to go bowling later that night.

Nearby, Linda and Dennis Lunsford were watching the weather, trying to decide whether to go out to eat before or after the storm. On Minnie Street in southwest Wichita, Linda Levernez and her four children were waiting for Duane Levernez to bring home dinner. He had just gotten his paycheck from his job as a repairman. Down the street, Peggy and Clarence Gilbert, a retired couple, were listening intently to the weather warnings.

At the Cox Produce Farm and market on Seneca in Wichita preparations were under way to open the next day for what was expected to be a very successful 1991 season.

"The crops were the best we'd had in 20 years," says Ron Stein, whose maternal grandparents started the business 65 years ago.

An early spring with just the right amount of moisture and no hard freezes had made the family optimistic about the upcoming harvest. Stein and his father Charlie had just returned from Oklahoma City with a truckload of fruit to offer for sale. Ron's mother, Helen, and the rest of the family were finishing several days of work landscaping the area around their market and tidying the tree-lined driveway.

Few chores remained before opening, although the family had to deal with one irritation. The family's 8-year-old Shetland sheep dog, Moosie, kept running outdoors and barking at the sky. Ron's son, Ronnie Ray, had to

chase after Moosie several times that afternoon and pull her back inside to quiet her. But every time Moosie was left alone, she would break away, dash outside and bark fiercely at the sky.

At 5:57 p.m. white wisps of cloud whirled together to form a funnel and touch the ground south of Haysville near the town of Clearwater. Winds inside the funnel blew at 100 miles per hour as the tornado scooted to the northeast, cutting a path 300 feet wide.

Within minutes, winds inside the funnel intensified to speeds as high as 200 miles per hour. Several vortices snaked to the ground as the tornado uprooted trees and tore through one mobile home and then another. The tornado smashed into the 80-acre farm of Jack and Chelsea McCreery. In seconds, almost $1 million worth of equipment and buildings was destroyed.

Haysville Police Lt. John Coleman was driving through Timber Lane when the report came over his radio that a tornado had been sighted nearby. As the Haysville town sirens sounded around him, Coleman was ordered to drive out of town to find the tornado. Coleman met up with it just outside the city limits. At first, he could not tell whether it was on the ground or in the sky.

"I got closer to it and I could see all the debris getting churned up into the air," Coleman says.

Coleman reported the sighting and then picked up his camera. Shooting frames as he drove, Coleman followed the funnel as it swirled past the town's water tower and fire station.

The tornado came within one mile of an industrial complex, narrowly missing an electrical generating station and three chemical plants.

Ron Stein, co-owner of Cox Produce Farm and market. says his family was optimistic about the season before the tornado appeared. Photo by Trish Birk

Haysville Police Lt. John Coleman was looking east on 71st Street when he took this photo. The water tower is to the right of the road.

Right: Work began almost immediately after the tornado on Sandy and Duane Free's home in Haysville after the tornado struck During the tornado, Sandy and her children hid under a pool table in the basement. Photo by Police Lt. John Coleman

*"It looked like birds were flying all around, coming at us."*

–Donna Tobler

At the Tobler house in Timber Lane the telephone rang, and Donna Tobler answered. It was her 19-year-old son, Kelly, warning her that a tornado had been sighted near Clearwater. But as Donna hung up all she could see through the patio windows was a heavy downpour of rain and hailstones bouncing off the ground. Donna was looking out the window when Tony came into the room.

"I told Tony, 'God! look at that hail coming down," she says. "In just a matter of seconds it got real still. I had a real weird feeling inside. Everything was so quiet. It was like everything went dead."

Donna walked to the living room door and pulled it open. "I don't know why," she says. Donna looked out.

"It looked like birds were flying all round, coming at us."

But it wasn't birds. It was debris. Two blocks away, the funnel was roaring towards them.

Tony came to the door and shouted, "Donna, get the kids and get to the basement. That's a tornado."

Donna took the children downstairs, Tony following. As he ran, he looked back over his shoulder and saw a neighbor's roof fly off.

Huddled in the basement, they listened. They heard a fierce wind blowing and windows breaking.

The tornado traveled away from the Tobler house. Witnesses saw at least three vortices fingering the ground.

Nearby, Dennis Lunsford decided it was time to bring the dog, Sam, inside the house. As he stepped outside, he spotted the funnel. Dennis hurried inside with Sam, shouting at Linda to go to the basement. Linda saw a tree break and stood watching, mesmerized by the sight.

She thought, "I've never seen a tornado before." Linda finally headed for the basement. They made it underground moments before the house was hit.

"I heard all the windows break, a big boom as the roof went," Linda says.

Nearby, Sandy Free had been listening to weather reports ever since she had arrived home from her job with an accounting firm. When the sirens sounded, she hurried her children, Joshua, 8, and Aaron, 4, into the basement. They crawled under the pool table.

"Then we started really knowing we'd been hit," Sandy says. "We were seeing the insulation coming downstairs at us."

Huddled beside his mother, Joshua feared for their safety.

"We're goners," Joshua said.

"I kept saying, 'We're okay. God's watching out for us.'"

The tornado tracked out of Haysville and headed northeast to a 40-acre field full of young vegetable plants at the Cox Farm.

The family was unloading the truck filled with fruit when Ron Stein looked up and saw the tornado coming. At first, he thought it was going to miss them.

The top of the tornado darkened the sky. Debris churned up from its base obscured the bottom of the funnel. Rain poured down and then hail. Seconds later, the tornado hit the farm.

Ron and 18 others — mostly family members who own or work at the market — rushed to a storm shelter on their property. Even the dog Moosie made it inside.

"It sounded like everything just went down all at once

— a big loud explosion," Ron says. "Trees fell over the door."

The tornado hopscotched on. A trailer court and trailer-sales company on opposite sides of 57th Street and South Broadway were demolished.

On Minnie Street, the Gilberts were disagreeing about whether they should immediately seek shelter in the storm cellar at their son's house, which was only a few blocks away. Clarence wanted to leave. Peggy wasn't ready to go yet.

"I told him I was going to hurry and do dishes before," Peggy says. "I put them in the drainer and then we went up."

Ten minutes before the tornado arrived, the couple finally got into their car and drove to the home of their son, Clarence Jr., and his wife, Pamela. Even then they did not take cover immediately. Clarence and Pamela stood outside the fruit cellar that served as the tornado shelter and watched the storm approach. Clarence Jr. yelled at them to get downstairs. Pamela replied that she had never seen a tornado before. As she watched, two funnels approached the house. When they met and formed one tornado, all the Gilberts ran down the steps to the fruit cellar.

"That's when we got hit," Peggy says. The family sat on milk crates in the cellar with their heads tucked down.

"It didn't last long, about 30 seconds," Peggy says. "I was scared to death."

Down Minnie Street, the Levernez children were picking up their toys and cleaning the house in preparation for their father's arrival home. Linda turned on the television as she always did when the sky looks threatening. "It just kind of got strange looking," Linda says.

As the television weatherman continued to emphasize the danger, sirens sounded. Linda took her kids into a walk-in closet that connects two bedrooms. There is a door on each end of the closet. They pulled storage boxes out of the way, took pillows from the couch and made a protective nest inside

"My kids and I got together and we said a prayer. We just asked for God's protection."

Linda told her children to stay inside the closet. "I went and looked out the door. There wasn't much to see except a rainstorm."

She sat on the couch, watching the weather reports on TV. Suddenly, everything outside the house was very still.

The TV weatherman warned, "If you're sitting on the couch watching me, you need to be in some kind of cover."

She stood up. The television blinked and went off. She hadn't touched it. As she went to the bedroom closet, Linda glanced out a window. The wind was bending the trees over so far they nearly laid on the ground. She saw a neighbor sprint through the yard to his house. Hurrying into the closet, Linda turned to close the door. The wind slammed it shut in front of her. She picked up her 1-year-old daughter and sat down. The younger children gathered around her. Linda's 10-year-old daughter Nancy was sitting on the other side of the closet near the second door.

The family was surrounded by a roar that kept growing louder and louder. To calm her children, Linda talked to them.

Clearence Gilbert and his wife Peggy sought shelter in the fruit cellar at their son's house. Photo by Trish Birk.

15

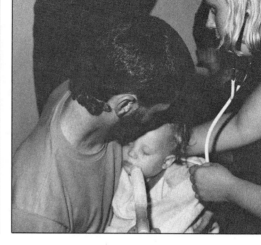

One trailer is tumbled against another in the Harbor Trailer Court. Photo by Kenneth Kocher.

Right: Stuart Smith (left) and his wife Rhonda (right) treat their son Jared (center) with a breathing machine and the help of the Red Cross, which supplied the electricity to run the machine at their Haysville shelter. Jared, who has asthma, was released from the hospital a few hours before the tornado cut the power to the Smiths' home. Photo by LuVerne Paine.

Linda Levernez and her children rode out the tornado in a closet in their home in Wichita. Photo by Roberta Birk.

"I said we're going to be OK. I kept telling them we're going to be OK. When it got so loud we almost couldn't talk to one another, I said that's what a tornado sounds like."

Linda says she could hear things hitting the house. "It was deafening. My ears were popping from the pressure," she says.

Suddenly, the door near Nancy popped open and banged into her. The girl screamed and cried, "Mommie!" Burdened by the baby, Linda tried to reach Nancy, but could not move fast enough. Nancy leaned against the door, shoved it shut and lay down on the floor. Huddled on her side, Nancy blocked the door from opening.

Pressure from the tornado's whirling winds built and Linda began to worry. Perhaps, they were going to die, she thought.

"It was an awful feeling. I felt like I was being squeezed."

A groan came from the house around them. "All of a sudden the house went whomp," she says.

The pressure eased up. The closet door near Linda popped opened. Linda saw the tornado move across the north edge of Peggy and Clarence Gilbert's yard.

"It was white and it was full of paper. I can remember the paper, like sheets of white paper. Behind the tornado was a rainbow.

"I felt like, well, that was God's promise that it's not coming back. And I told the kids when the door opened, 'That's what a tornado looks like.' And nobody moved."

In the Timber Lane section of Haysville, the Toblers and their children picked their way upstairs through the debris. They found broken glass, overturned plants and debris scattered across the floor. They were relieved. Somehow it seemed they had missed the worst of the storm.

Tony opened the door that led to the garage and yelled, 'Where's my garage?'

Little remained standing, but one thing was untouched — the glass Tony had left behind still sat on the bench, full of water.

The Toblers walked out and looked around. Every house west of their home was destroyed. Police roadblocks would delay the family of the last child left in Donna's day care, C.J. Ashley, for quite a while. Once C.J.'s father, Winston, made it in, "he was just thankful C.J. was OK," Donna says.

The Ashleys returned the next day to help the Toblers begin the long task of cleaning up.

At the Lunsford house, Linda and Dennis and the dog Sam emerged and discovered that their roof had vanished. Two vehicles parked in their garage were demolished. A third was badly damaged. A battered gray Cavalier, a neighbor's car, rested on the ground near one side of the house.

"The tornado picked the gray car up, spun it around and hit the side of my house," Linda says.

When Sandy Free and her children climbed to the ground level, they found that many of their belongings had disappeared. A bedroom set and a couch had been whisked away.

"It was chaos, just total chaos," Sandy says. "It left little things, but took huge things, little things that had

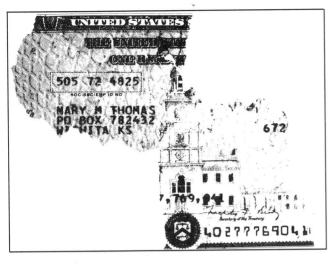

been on the dresser were still in the room."

But the dresser, a hutch and mirror had vanished. "It didn't even shatter my windows," Sandy says.

The next morning, a woman who lived several blocks away returned Sandy's purse.

At the Cox Farm, Ron Stein and his family discovered that they were trapped. The door to the storm shelter was jammed shut.

Ron and his cousin Leon raised the door about a foot, enough to allow Leon's children, Bo, 13, and Jake, 16, to squeeze out and run for help. In the shelter, people began to notice the odor of natural gas. The odor was nauseating. The people in the shelter began to develop headaches.

"The gas meter had broken," Ron says. "It was about 30 feet from the cellar and gas was coming right down in the shelter."

After 20 minutes people came and lifted branches and debris from the cellar door. Helen Stein says they never learned the identity of their rescuers.

"They ran on down the street to see if they could help somebody else," Helen says.

The release of the family from the shelter brought little relief as they looked in disbelief at their surroundings. Debris from the house was piled 20 feet high. Nothing else remained.

"No buildings, no nothing," Ron says. "Everything was flat. Not one wall. From there, I think I went into shock. You don't know what to do."

On Minnie Street, the Gilberts survived in their son's basement. When they finally made it home they discovered that the tornado had lifted their house off its concrete-block foundation. Some of the blocks were scattered around their yard. Inside the house, the floors had caved in. An outside wall bowed out. A window that had been in that wall was inside the house. The window was intact, without so much as a cracked pane.

In their yard, the Gilberts found a microwave oven, a refrigerator full of food and a dishwasher. They had never seen any of the appliances before. The Gilberts' own washing machine and dryer stayed put in their utility room, but the dryer was filled with glass. The washer was packed with grass, mud, fiberglass and wheat, presumably from a field two blocks away.

At the Levernez house, Linda told the children to stay in the closet as she checked the house. A mist of dust was drifting in the house like a fog. She was amazed at the amount of light in the house, although the roof was intact, then Linda realized the garage was gone.

"There had been a garage there and it had blocked two windows and that was why there was so much light," she says. "I could see the trees and the power lines down."

Her car, which had been parked in front of the garage, had been pushed halfway into where the garage had been, she says. The windshield was broken and the metal dented, but otherwise the car was intact.

Duane arrived home moments later. "He was so scared," Linda says. "The first thing he said was, 'The kids, the kids.'...The kids were crying because they were worried about their Daddy...I didn't know if he was caught in it."

Behind the Levernez house, there was a pile of debris as tall as their roof. Two trailer houses nearby sat in

*"No buildings, no nothing. Everything was flat. Not one wall. From there, I think I went into shock. You don't know what to do."*

–Ron Stein

Dianne, Jon and Josh Coats standing in what used to be the other half of their home in the River Oaks Mobile Home Park. Photo by Tony Smith.

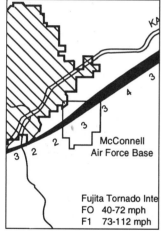

McConnell
Air Force Base

Fujita Tornado Inte
FO  40-72 mph
F1  73-112 mph

Numbers indicate strength on the Fujita scale.

another neighbor's yard.

"The tornado just picked them up and wadded them up and threw them in the back of their yard in just a massive heap," she says.

# The Big One: McConnell Air Force Base & Southeast Wichita

As the tornado rumbled toward the neighborhoods of south Wichita, television announcers urged people to take cover. Sirens blared on city streets and among the barracks and runways of neighboring McConnell Air Force Base. Telephones rang as friends warned friends of the danger.

At Meyers Garden Spot Nursery and Greenhouse at 53rd and Hydraulic streets, owner Elliott Redenbaugh, his wife Nellie and Gloria Hardesty were at work in the concrete block building that housed the nursery's office. The telephone rang. Hardesty answered. It was Bob Lawler, an employee who had just left work. He was calling from home two miles away.

"Gloria, get out of the building," Lawler said. "I can see the tornado from here!"

Elliott Redenbaugh looked out the front door and saw the boiling storm cloud and shouted a warning. Elliott, Nellie and Hardesty yelled to another employee and the customers he was helping — a young couple with three children. All ran for the cellar.

"We were there maybe a minute and a half before it hit," Hardesty says. "I felt like the suction was pulling everything out of me."

The people who lived in the trailers were not at home, nor were most of the other neighbors.

"We were very lucky," Linda says. "No one died on our street." △

At the River Oaks Mobile Home Park across the street, Dianne Coats came home from work to find her three children praying. Even though no tornado was in sight, they were frightened because they had once before had a close call with a funnel, Coats says.

"They knew it was important to pray during times like that," she says.

Her husband telephoned from work at the Dillard Department Store in Towne East square mall and reported that a tornado had been sighted 20 miles from their home. He urged his wife and children to stay together and not go anywhere. Thinking that the tornado was too far away to threaten them, Coats decided not to go immediately to the park's storm shelter.

Moment's later, her 13-year-old daughter Alicia turned away from the television.

"Mom, where do we live?" Alicia asked. " Do we live in south Wichita?"

"Yes, we do."

"The TV says there's a tornado in south Wichita."

Coats walked with Alicia to the door and looked out. A strange cloud was roiling toward them.

Left: The tornado moved the car from one side of Lee William's house to the other. Photo by Lee Williams.

When the tornado struck, this vehicle was parked in the McConnell Air Force Base hospital parking lot on Rock Road. Photo by Major Mike Hunsucker.

"What is that?" Coats asked.

Alicia replied, "That's the tornado!"

Coats rushed the children to the back bedroom of their mobile home. She told the children to lay on top of the waterbed and she squatted beside it, holding a toddler who was visiting that afternoon. "We heard it coming," Coats says.

In the Cottage Grove-Oaklawn area, Cheryl Contreras, her neighbor Shereen Wilson and their five children and Contreras' grandchild grabbed pillows and blankets and hurried toward a hallway in Contreras' house after a warning from television. All except Contreras ran inside the hallway, covered themselves and waited. Contreras lingered just outside the hallway for a minute to watch for the tornado.

"I saw it go up, and then all of a sudden I saw debris in front of the house and I dove for the hallway myself," she says.

They were engulfed by the roar of what sounded like a freight train. They held onto each other and screamed. Glass shattered around them.

Several blocks to the northeast, Lee Williams, an aviation technician, did not think twice about the rumbling roar he heard. Like other neighborhood residents, Williams was accustomed to the window-shaking sounds of B-1 bombers taking off from the nearby air base.

Suddenly, his neighbor Ron White ran through the front door, yelling, "It's coming! It's coming now!"

Williams says, "Then I knew what the sound was. I just pointed at the closet I kept empty so we'd have a place to go in case of a tornado."

Williams, his 8-year-old son Justin, White, his wife and two sons crowded into the closet. Williams's 10-year-old son Nick did not follow them. Nick stood motionless near the front. Williams' 12-year-old son, Chris, was not in sight.

"I kept yelling to Nick to get into the closet," Williams says.

But the words were drowned out by the roar of the tornado, then Williams saw Chris. He was hanging onto the front door frame.

"I hollered at him but I knew he couldn't hear me either," Williams says. "I could tell the wind was tearing him up. I think he hung on there for about 4 or 5 seconds, and then he was gone."

Williams started to run after Chris, but the closet door slammed shut in front of him. "I just got all empty inside," Williams says.

Northeast of Lee Williams' house, Jae and Sun Hong were sitting in their yard with relatives. Natives of Korea, the Hongs had only been in the United States for four years. They had never seen a tornado. As they talked, the Hongs watched the clouds southwest of them begin to boil wildly.

"We watched it, and we were laughing and saying 'What is it? What is it?" Sun says.

Their 14-year-old nephew, Dail Hong, ran out of the house.

"It's not funny!" Dail yelled. "It's a tornado. We have to get to the basement."

The family rushed downstairs, and neighbors from a nearby mobile home joined them in the basement. An instant later, the roar was upon them. "It sounded like a

Sun Hong and her daughter Susan stand on their newly repaired front porch. The old porch was lost in the storm. Photo by Carol Duerksen.

Two cars are jammed into the main entrance of the McConnell Air Force Base hospital. Only the underside of the car on the left is visible. Photo by Airman 1st Class Jason White.

Wing weather officer 1st Lt. Frederick Williams was one of the base meteorologists who predicted and then witnessed the tornado. Photo by Carol Duerksen.

big bomb," Sun says.

At McConnell, Staff Sgt. Mike Snell and Sgt. Jim Williams were working in its airport control tower. They had already heard reports of tornadoes striking throughout south-central Kansas.

Snell spotted the funnel first. It was 8 miles away, partially hidden behind the huge Boeing plant. Snell jumped onto a ledge for a better view and clearly saw the funnel, debris flying around it.

"We called the base weather people and told them what we'd seen," Snell says. "We watched it, and knew it was coming toward the base."

The base sounded its sirens. It was 6:10 p.m. Soon afterwards, Maj. Mike Hunsucker, commander of the base Weather Squadron, watched the tornado rumble across the base runways. The funnel was "pure white," Hunsucker says.

"We weren't feeling fear, as much as just helplessness," he says. "It was something to behold. I kept thinking, 'I can't believe it's going to hit us.'"

Wing weather officer 1st Lt. Frederick Williams was angry.

"It's one thing to be out as a weather spotter, and you feel in control because you know where it is and where you can go. But when you've got it coming at your face and you can't move, it made me mad because I felt so helpless."

As the funnel rumbled toward the weather station, the men took cover under desks in the center of the building.

Williams and another member of the forecasting team, Airman 1st Class Tony Barnier, headed for the bathroom. They sat on the floor and put chairs over their heads for protection. Barnier joked about how wonderful this was. Williams laughed. "Will you shut up? I'm trying to pray." The tornado passed within 220 yards of the building.

At the nearby Towne East square mall, Sgt. Mike Cooter, Airman 1st Class Scott Rose and Senior Airman Corey Arellano of McConnell's Security Police Squadron were enjoying a night off duty. But when they heard reports of a tornado, they headed for the base. By the time they reached the east gate near the Visitors Center, the three men could clearly see the tornado coming towards them. About a dozen people appeared confused as they searched for shelter near the gate. At first, the men discussed telling everyone to get in a nearby ditch.

"But then we noticed the electrical wires and transformer overhead," Cooter says,

The three men told the people to head for the Visitors Center. The three followed them inside. The tornado crossed Rock Road.

The funnel passed within 2,000 yards of more than 80 military jets parked on the base runways. Everything from B-1B bombers, F-16 fighters and KC-135 tankers sat on the runway that day. The local newspaper, *The Wichita Eagle*, later reported that at least two B-1Bs were loaded with nuclear warheads. Later the Air Force would not comment on whether the planes contained nuclear weapons.

The tornado thundered through the base arts and crafts center, the Non-Commissioned Officers Club, the sports center, the community center, a credit union,

Left: Four months after the tornado, J.C. Pruitt surveys the ruin of his yard near Pawnee and Greenwich. Photo by Carol Duerksen.

The devastation is still evident in Wichita. Photo by Marsha Callaway.

bowling alley and the base hospital. The tornado smashed 110 family homes and the base's school, Wineteer Elementary School. Burger King, the base exchange, the dining hall, day-care center and a bank were all damaged.

At base housing, Kim Nowicki, the wife of a member of the Security Police Squadron, and her 8-year-old daughter Dianne heard the sirens. Kim's husband, Edward, was not at home. Dianne was outside, but she quickly ran back into the house.

"There's a twister at the base," Dianne shouted.

Kim Nowicki looked out the window and spotted the tornado. "It was big and white," she says.

Nowicki took her daughter into the bathroom of their single-story house, but then she worried that the house would never withstand the force of a tornado. Nowicki grabbed her car keys, intending to drive them to safety. But once outside the house she realized that it was too late to flee.

"We decided to run across the street to another house — a two-story house," Nowicki says. But panic took over and the two stood in the center of the street. "I don't know what I was thinking," Nowicki says.

Across the street, Michael Kindred had just gotten his two children into the safety of the bathroom.

"I thought it was the safest place in the house," he says. Kindred looked out his front door and saw the tornado approaching.

"I knew it was headed directly for us," he says. "Then I saw a woman and her daughter outside. I yelled at them to come to our house."

Nowicki and her daughter did not move.

"I reacted," Kindred says. "It was just instinct."

He ran to the street, grabbed Dianne and shouted, 'Run! Go!' But they were 50 yards from his house.

"I didn't think we could make it," Kindred says. Instead, they sprinted to a neighbor's house and pounded on the door.

A 17-year-old girl and her little brother let them in. All of them hurried to the bathroom. The tornado was half a block away.

In the bathroom, the roar of the tornado surrounded them. Kindred prayed for his children.

Nowicki says, "My daughter and I were screaming. I could feel the wall behind my back moving in and out, in and out."

The tornado rumbled out of the base and headed northeast.

Near the intersection of Pawnee and Greenwich streets, J.C. Pruitt and his family were watching the weather warnings on television. The weatherman announced that the twister had damaged the Air Force base. Minutes later, Pruitt saw the roof fly off his neighbor's house. He grabbed a flashlight and shouted to his wife and three grandchildren to follow him. Pruitt thought they were behind him as he ran to the storm cellar in the yard.

"I couldn't lift the plywood that was over the outdoor cellar," Pruitt says. "The wind was too strong. I just barely slid the plywood over and crawled in. Then the garage flew over the cellar."

Inside the cellar, Pruitt realized that his wife and grandchildren had not followed him.

Nearby on Richfield Street, Marsha and Noble

*"My daughter and I were screaming. I could feel the wall behind my back moving in and out, in and out."*

– Kim Nowicki

About 5 minutes before the tornado struck, this was the scene from Sharon and Gary Siegrist's driveway on Creekside Court in Wichita. Photo by Gary Siegrist

Right: The tornado lifted the tops off the greenhouses at Meyer's Garden Spot Nursery and Greenhouse, Photo by Gloria Hardesty.

*"About that time, the front door sucked shut and it made the most awful moaning noise, and the air sucking through it."*

–Marsha Callaway

Callaway heard the sirens.

"It didn't look that bad and it hadn't rained very much at all," Marsha says.

They turned on the radio. Within seconds, the radio reported that the tornado had been sighted at McConnell. A noise that sounded like jet engines filled their home.

"About that time, the front door sucked shut and it made the most awful moaning noise, and the air sucking through it. Then there was no doubt," Marsha says.

Marsha headed to the bedroom and picked up her purse. Her husband grabbed her and brought her to the center of their house. Noble pushed her under a large built-in desk that was sheltered by closets on both sides.

"It was only seconds before it was tearing into the house," Marsha says. "It just sounded like one of those B1-B bombers, terrible, crashing and glass. A car ended up in our bedroom and rolled on out."

In the same neighborhood, Mathilda Bebout may or may not have heard the warnings. No one knows. Neighbor Gloria Capps saw Mathilda out in her yard. Mathilda appeared to be searching for her beloved Rottweiler, Sam.

Gloria and her husband Clarence had just returned home from an aborted trip to a high school dinner. The weather had seemed too threatening to stay away from home. After arriving back at their house, the couple changed into casual clothing. Gloria put a pot of soup on the stove. They were aware of the weather warnings, but they did not take action until Clarence looked out of the southwest window. The tornado was only 200 yards away. The air was filled with debris — trees, rooftops, a car, a boat and a boat trailer. There was no sound, Clarence says.

Clarence called to Gloria, "If we're going to go anyplace, we better go."

He grabbed Gloria's hand and the two darted to a bedroom to pick up pillows, then they went to a hallway in the center of the house.

"I tried to close the door to the hall," Gloria says. The wind grabbed the door out of her hand and flung it open. Around them, glass was breaking, wood splintering. Gloria thought to herself, "I can't believe this is happening."

A few blocks away amid the roar and flying debris, Charlene Montgomery was trying to reach the shelter of a neighbor's basement with her teenaged daughter Keri and her nieces, 5-year-old Anna Cravens and 2-year-old Susan Cravens. The tornado engulfed them and then moved to the northeast.

At 143rd and Kellogg streets, Paula Bruce and her husband Herb, a real estate developer, were rounding up their cats.

A wide black funnel broke through a nearby belt of sheltering trees. The funnel was whirling and churning debris. Paula, Herb, their two cats and two German shepherds ran down the steps to a basement bathroom.

"It was like a big jet flying into us at full power," Paula says. "We felt the air pressure drop and our ears filled and crackled. When we heard a noise like a freight train going over a wooden trestle, we knew it was right on top of us. Everything started shaking, including our knees."

Above them came the sound of a loud clattering, like

Left: Marsha Callaway's daughter, Lana (just right of center), searches the remains of Marsha's house for salvagable items. Photo by Marsha Callaway.

Cheryl Contreras' house sustained extensive damage.

metal trays being poured down a tin chute, Paula says.

"There was the sound of nails being violently ripped from wood, and lumber clacking against lumber," Paula says.

In no more than 20 seconds, it was over. The tornado rumbled north, straight for Andover.

At Meyers Garden Spot Nursery and Greenhouse on Hydraulic Street, owners Nellie and Elliott Redenbaugh, employee Gloria Hardesty, another employee, and their customers climbed out of their storm cellar and looked around in disbelief.

"It didn't seem possible so much destruction could happen in such a short time," Hardesty says.

The office building, 12 greenhouses, a two-story house and nine vehicles had all been destroyed.They looked across the street at the River Oaks Mobile Home Park. "Oh no!" They cried.

In the mobile home park, Dianne Coats opened the door of the bedroom where she had hidden with her children. She gazed out into the sky. The other half of their trailer had vanished.

"The trailers around us had disappeared, just gone," Coats says.

Her 9-year-old son Jon looked where his bedroom had been and exclaimed, "My baseball cards!" Alicia said, "Mom, we're still here!" All the Coatses, including their 2-year-old guest, had survived.

At the Towne East mall, Hartlan Coats walked out of the storm shelter and learned that a tornado had torn through Wichita. When he heard a report that the storm

had hit Meyers Nursery and the neighboring trailer park, Hartlan bolted for his car.

"I headed home, and every time the horrible thoughts of what could have happened to my family came to mind, I pushed them out," he says. "Deep down inside I had the peace of God and knew they were OK."

Hartlan got to 47th and Hydraulic before he was stopped by debris in the street. He covered the next three blocks on foot, but was stopped by a police barricade.

"They told me that they had rescue personnel in there bringing people out and taking them to White Elementary School," he says.

Hartlan ran into the mother of the 2-year-old who had been spending the afternoon with his family. Together they went to the school. They met one of his sons' teachers who said she had been inside River Oaks and had seen his sons digging in the rubble. The teacher knew nothing about Hartlan's wife and daughter. Hartlan stood and watched people from the mobile home park walking to the school.

"Their faces reflected the devastation they'd just seen," Hartlan says. "They looked like they'd been to a funeral and walked past the casket and had broken down crying and screaming."

Suddenly, the looks of devastation turned to terror. Authorities said another tornado was on its way. Hartlan started to run for shelter in the school, but then he stopped. "I saw my family coming down the street toward me." In a few minutes, the tornado warning was canceled.

In the Cottage Grove-Oaklawn area, Cheryl Contreras

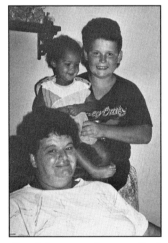

Cheryl Contreras, her son Chad Herren, and granddaughter Karisa Herren made it through the tornado without suffering even a scratch. Photo by Carol Duerksen.

23

No one was badly hurt despite the fact that the roof was torn off these family housing units at McConnell Air Force Base. Many people were hiding in hallways and closets. Photo by Tim C. Sutton.

Right: Family housing units on McConnell Air Force Base were gutted by the tornado. Photo by Victor Trisvan.

*"She'd had a pillow over her head and there were feathers all over her."*

Airman 1st Class Scott Rose

,her children and grandchild, her neighbor Shereen Wilson and her children emerged from the hallway of the Contreras home. Under their feet were shards of glass. None of them was even scratched.

Around them, the furnishings were ruined. Feathers had been sucked off the family parrot. The family discovered a red dress Contreras' teen-aged daughter Angie planned to wear to the upcoming prom. The dress was hanging untouched from Angie's bedroom door. The bedroom wall sagged outward and debris littered the floor.

Outside the house, trees had been snapped and uprooted. Two heavy wooden benches were broken in half. Strangest of all, the tornado had deposited barbecue grills — 16 of them — in the backyard.

Lee Williams, his family and neighbors, were emerging from the closet where they had taken refuge. In his mind, Williams could still see his 12-year-old son Chris being blown away in the wind and his 10-year-old son Nick standing dazed in the living room.

Williams pushed the closet door open and there was Nick, still standing in the living room.

"The ceiling had fallen around and on him, but he wasn't hurt."

Williams went outside to look for Chris. His son called to him. The boy was at the front of the porch. His leg was injured, but not severely.

The car Williams had parked on the south side of his house was now on the north side of the house. The car was a tangled ruin.

On 31st South, the Hongs climbed out of their basement and found their home damaged but standing.

All the windows were broken, and the porch had vanished. Trash filled their yard.

On the Air Force base, the weather forecasters, all safe, looked at the destruction around them. Sgt. Mike Cooter, Airman 1st Class Scott Rose and Senior Airman Corey Arellano emerged unharmed from the Visitors Center.

First, Cooter, Rose and Arellano went to check on a friend's family at base housing. The friend's home had been demolished but the family was fine. Arellano took the family to the youth center where Base Disaster Recovery had headquarters, while the other two men started a house-to-house search for victims. They entered an area filled with the smell of a gas and heard a teen-aged girl screaming for help.

"I yelled for Sgt. Cooter, and we both went in together," Rose says. "We found her in what had been the bathroom with a sink on top of her and water spraying in her face. She'd had a pillow over her head and there were feathers all over her."

The two men pulled debris away from the teenager and reassured her that she would be fine. The girl was in pain from an injured leg. When medics arrived to take her to the hospital, the two men resumed their search.

"I really didn't want to go into any more houses," Rose says. "After finding that girl, it was really scary. I just didn't want that situation to happen again." Fortunately, they found no more victims.

Fortunately, they found no more victims. When the second tornado warning was issued, the men once again helped people find shelter. Scrambling through rain and hail, Rose ran into a guy wire and was momentarily

Left: Thirty-five years after Noble Callaway bought this Chevrolet, the tornado destroyed it. Photo by Marsha Callaway.

The desk that sheltered Marsha and Noble Callaway is directly behind the rubble in the center of the picture. That pile of rubble marks the area where Marsha originally sought shelter. Noble pulled her to safety. Photo by Marsha Callaway.

knocked unconscious. By the time the warning was cancelled, Rose's face was swollen, and he had bruises across his chest and arms. Sgt. Doug Harberson, another security officer, offered to drive Rose and Cooter to a hospital. At the intersection of Harry and Oliver they encountered the aftermath of a traffic accident, A man was hunched in front of a pickup truck.

"No one was stopping to help," Cooter says." The only person there was the guy who'd been driving the truck, and he was in a panic and didn't know what to do."

While Cooter ran to summon an ambulance, Rose and Harberson applied first aid to the victim.

"The guy's head was bleeding bad, and then he went into shock," Rose says. "We just did what we could until the paramedics got there." .

At base housing, Michael Kindred and Kim and Dianne Nowicki left their hiding place as soon as the tornado passed. Kindred ran out of the house and sprinted to his own home where he had left his children when he dashed out to help Nowicki and her daughter.

"God, let my kids be OK," Kindred prayed as he ran. His children survived uninjured, although the house was damaged.

At the Nowicki house, the roof and wall had fallen into the bathroom and hallway where Nowicki had first thought to take shelter with her daughter.

"I really don't think we would have lived through it in that bathroom," Nowicki says.

At the intersection of Pawnee and Greenwich, J. C. Pruitt emerged from the storm cellar and saw that every house on his block was gone except his own. He ran to check on his family. All had stayed in the house. Other

than a cut on Pruitt's head, there were no injuries, but practically everything on his property was damaged.

Before the tornado, Pruitt's backyard had been a haven for his hobbies. It had housed guinea fowl, ducks, beehives, several small buildings and a camper. Large trees had shaded the yard.

After the tornado, the yard was filled with twisted, jagged trees, dead baby guineas and the tangled wreckage of his camper. Hundreds of bees buzzed through the air.

Not far from the Pruitt house, Marsha and Noble Callaway were emerging from their hiding place under the desk. Their roof was gone.

"I could smell cedar very strong," Marsha says. "We had a cedar tree south of the house, and I knew that tree was in the house, and it was."

When they walked outside the first thing the two saw was a treasured 1956 Chevrolet that Noble had owned since he bought it in 1956.

"He was going to redo it when he retired," Marsha says.

The car was wrapped around a tree. A two-story barn the Callaways had built with their house was gone. Noble's tractor was demolished, lying upside down in the yard.

"We looked across the street and the house across from us was completely gone," Marsha says. "There wasn't a wall or fixture or a pipe."

Marsha walked into the road and turned around and looked at what was left of her home.

"I went down to my knees," Marsha says. "A neighbor helped me to my feet and said, 'Thank God,

Marsha and Noble Callaway survived by taking cover under this desk, which was built into a wall. Photo by Marsha Callaway.

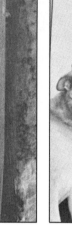

This nail was driven head first into a tree that was stripped of its bark by the tornado. Photo by Mike Hunsucker.

Right: Craig Reiserer sits with his dogs Tiger (left) and Beau (right). The tornado carried the dogs about 1/2 mile through the air. Photo by Carol Duerksen.

The tornado sheared away the east wall of this house on Greenwich. Photo by Mikel Lewis.

you are alive.'"

Everyone in Marsha's immediate block survived. The people who lived in the house across the street left before the tornado hit.

At what was left of the Capps house, Gloria and Clarence Capps were coming to consciousness. Gloria was face down on the ground 50 feet from the house. A closet door and a mattress were stacked on her back. She had one shoe on and one shoe off. Clarence had been thrown 80 feet from the house. As he looked around, Clarence realized that all the houses and the trees were gone.

"If you had asked me right then who I was, I don't believe I could have told you," Clarence says. "I really didn't know where I was for a few seconds."

He panicked because he couldn't see Gloria, then he heard her hollering for help. Clarence followed the screams until he found Gloria. He pulled off the mattress and the door. Gloria's arm was bleeding. She had huge bruises around her eye, thigh, hand and back. Clarence suffered a cut on his ear and a badly bruised shoulder and rib.

The couple hobbled down Greenwich Road for several blocks before they found a ride to the hospital.

Near the Cappses house, searchers found the bodies of Charlene Montgomery and her nieces Anna and Susan Cravens. Montgomery's daughter Keri survived, but her back had been broken by the storm.

For people with relatives in the neighborhood, the aftermath of the storm was an agonizing journey through debris-clogged roads and police roadblocks.

When he heard that the tornado had hit his mother's neighborhood, Doug Bebout, Mathilda Bebout's son, immediately went to check on her.

In his first attempt to reach her home, police stopped him at a barricade. When he finally got in, Doug discovered the debris that had once been his mother's home. There was no sign of his mother.

Doug and his brother, Walter, contacted every hospital in the city. Seven hours after the tornado, Walter identified the body of a woman at St. Joseph Medical Center as his mother, Mathilda Bebout.

Neighborhood residents who were at work when the tornado struck also faced frustration and fear. Although they had missed the terror of being in the tornado, they did not know if their homes still existed or if their pets had survived.

Lance Darling, restaurant supervisor at the Marriott Hotel, and Ray Macheda, the hotel's executive chef, owned a house near Pawnee and Greenwich. Before leaving for work that morning, Darling had difficulty getting Macheda's dog, a Samoyed husky, to go outside. The dog normally stayed outside, but balked this time at the idea of leaving the house. Finally the dog went outside.

While the tornado moved through the center of their neighborhood, the two men watched the funnel from the lobby of the hotel. Darling was the first of the two to attempt a trip home.

He drove until his passage was blocked by debris, then he got out and ran. He ran, in fact, past his own block. "I didn't even recognize it," Darling says.

He backtracked and then he saw what had once been his house.

"It wasn't there anymore," Darling says. "The only thing I could think of was to look for the dog, but I couldn't find her either."

By this time, Macheda was on his way home. When he could not drive any farther, he too got out of his car and ran.

"I never run," Macheda says. "But I did then. When I got to the house, I was appalled. It looked like war had hit." That night Macheda found the body of the dog.

Craig Reiserer was at work at Eddy's Toyota in Wichita where he is the general manager when he heard that a tornado was ravaging south Wichita. He headed home immediately and arrived moments after the storm had passed through. The landscape was devastated.

"Neighbors were just coming out of their basements and everyone was in shock," Reiserer says.

His home was nothing more than a pile of rubble. His dogs, Tiger, a German Shepherd-Husky mix, and Beau, a large black Labrador, had been inside the house. Craig asked neighbors if they had seen the dogs. No one had. About an hour later, a car came by and slowed to a stop. The driver asked, "Is anybody here missing a couple of dogs?"

Reiserer hurried with the driver to a spot half a mile from his home. He was told that people standing in a courtyard had seen two dogs flying through the air with a tree and a refrigerator.

"They saw a big black dog land in the field and get up and run off," Reiserer says. "The other one hit the street in front of them."

When Craig arrived, Tiger was lying in the street in shock. She had a large puncture wound in her leg, but she was alive. Someone had covered her with a blanket.

Reiserer took Tiger to a veterinarian and then returned to the site of his home to look for Beau. By that time, it had gotten dark and rain was falling. Still wearing his business suit, Reiserer plodded through muddy fields, calling for his dog. At one point, he fell down in the field and cried from exhaustion and frustration.

Reiserer finally telephoned family and friends for help. In all, six people searched through the mud and debris with flashlights and Coleman lanterns. Reiserer picked up bits and pieces of his life, taking souvenirs and valuables from the mud as he searched. About 2 a.m., they gave up. After only a four-hour break, Reiserer headed back to resume the search. Driving up to the site of his house at 6 a.m., Reiserer saw Beau sitting on the front porch.

Never one to miss a meal, the black Labrador had already eaten a part of a 10-pound ham that had been in Reiserer's freezer. The freezer was nowhere in sight.

Dead silence greeted Paula Bruce and her husband Herb when they climbed out of their cellar. No insect chirped nor bird sang.

"We climbed out over the bricks, stood up and looked around and saw that all of our neighbors' homes were down too," Paula says. "The neighbors were climbing out of hiding too, and we all yelled at each other to find out if anyone was hurt."

Around them, the Bruces saw houses blown apart and turned into trash. Cars had been broken and thrown over the footings of a garage. A truck they had never seen before rested in their pond. The boat they kept in the pond had disappeared. The couple's truck was gone. Limbs and jagged fragments of trees were scattered

The tornado blackens as it heads toward Andover. This photo was taken a little after 6:30 p.m. on Augusta Airport Road, three miles east of Andover. Photo by Richard Parks

Right: The grandfather clock in Tollie Hartmann's house stopped at 6:40 p.m., the instant the tornado struck. Photo by Tollie Hartmann.

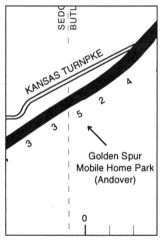

Numbers indicate strength on the Fujita scale.

across the ground. The pungent odor of sulphur and cedar filled the air. Bits of farm machinery had snagged in the jagged branches of the few trees that remained standing.

One of the Bruces' horses was lying on a pile of bricks. The other horse, Princess, was lying on a broken plate glass window. She was bleeding heavily.

"I kept wondering why there weren't sirens, or police checking on us," Paula says.

The couple heard siren after siren go by in the distance.

They heard glass tinkling, almost like a wind chime. It was the sound of Princess struggling on the glass window.

"Every time she moved, she drove a piece of glass in until I could see blood spurting from one of the wounds with every heartbeat," Paula says.

A sheriff's deputy arrived to check on the area. The deputy used his gun to end the horse's suffering.

"I couldn't watch, and I wish I hadn't heard the shot," Paula says.

The other horse had been able to stand, but was going into shock. The Bruces asked the neighbors to find anything warm to put over him. They covered the horse with an army blanket, a woman's coat and a child's blanket decorated with cartoon characters. Underneath it all, the horse stood absolutely still on top of a hill. He hung his head, his ears drooped.

In the distance, peacocks screamed their characteristic calls that sounded like, "Help! Help!"

# Andover & the Kansas Turnpike

The tornado intensified as it thundered toward its fatal assault on Andover, just east of Wichita.

With 4,047 residents, Andover is more of a bedroom community than an identifiable town. It is a mere four miles long and a little more than a mile wide in western Butler County, and it would be bisected by the growing funnel.

Residents, most with an ear cocked to their radios or televisions, proceeded on their usual Friday evening business. It was a mild evening, good for cooking out and relaxing after a week's work.

"It was a lovely night," says Tollie Hartmann, an electrical engineer. She lives in the Countryside Third Addition, a middle-class housing development in the middle of town. It was a nearly new neighborhood; Hartmann's family had been among the first residents in 1985 when they moved in.

That evening as she arrived home from work, Hartmann admired the way trees, shrubs and flowers had become established since then, and she thought, "Isn't this pretty?" The plants — and the homes they adorned — would be gone the next time she stepped outside.

For most in Andover, dinner was the priority. The

Rockstads, the Sargents, the Storrer girls and hundreds of others were doing what most people do between 6 and 6:30 on a Friday evening. They were eating. At Livingston's Restaurant, Joe Marks, was eating chicken fried steak and grousing, as usual, about the quality of the meal while he consumed every morsel.

It wasn't that they were complacent about the weather. Most knew about the tornado watch. They thought they knew how dangerous the storms are. But the evening just seemed so normal. A little cloudy, a little muggy, but it was April in Kansas, after all.

A few souls, however, seemed to understand what was yet unclear to the rest.

Harley, the Rockstads' family dog, was upset, running about anxiously in his home near Hartmann's as the Rockstads settled in for the evening.

Gladys Manes of Iowa, who was visiting her daughters, hadn't bothered to take her full kit with her when she and her husband, Robert Manes, had shifted from one daughter's home to the other. The home the Maneses had just arrived at was owned by their daughter, Mary Lou Spencer. Spencer's home was in Golden Spur Mobile Home Park, due east across Andover Road from the Countryside Third Addition. A relative called Gladys unexpectedly that afternoon just to talk, and throughout the day Gladys, kept telling people, "The Lord will take care of us."

That afternoon, Spencer was unexpectedly called to work the night shift at St. Francis Medical Center. Her departure from her trailer at Golden Spur left her frail parents alone.

As the storm drew near, some people were finishing their work day.

Russ Griffith is the pro and co-owner of the company that operates Green Valley Greens, Andover's municipal golf course. He was waiting for the last couple of golfers to leave. Rain had driven everyone else off the course, which borders the Sedgwick County line, and Griffith had heard sirens from eastern Wichita about 5 o'clock. When the final golfers at last checked out, Griffith drove away, heading for home.

Most people monitoring their televisions heard warnings of the tornado. News that it was heading for Andover was broadcast at least seven minutes before the tornado hit town, according to the National Weather Service.

Kathleen Long, didn't wait until then. She and her daughter, Beverly, had left their home in Golden Spur to seek shelter at their friends', the Mendozas', in the middle of the Countryside Third Addition. Beverly, 20, had always been very frightened of storms.

"She insisted we call a friend and go to their house with a basement," Long says.

Her Golden Spur neighbor Betty Parks also left. Parks, has a disability and must rest a lot. She was getting ready to lie down when her son called. He said, "Mother, are you dressed? I can see the storm coming. Get your clothes on and leave immediately."

So, Parks did, but she decided to go to a friend's house instead of to a nearby church as she had told her son during their telephone conversation. Her change in plans would later torment her family.

Throughout town, telephone lines were busy as friends and relatives passed on the tornado warnings.

Spencer, stuck at St. Francis Medical Center, called

Andover Police Sgt. Paul Troy See's squad car video camera captured a resident of Golden Spur Mobile Home Park who appears to be walking nonchalantly down the road 8 1/2 minutes before the tornado struck.

Right: After the cleanup, concrete foundations are the only sign remaining of many of the homes of Andover. Pizza Hut is visible in the top center of the photo. Across from Pizza Hut and a parking lot is the barren patch of ground where Livingston's Restaurant once stood.

PM 6:31:35

*"It kept getting larger and larger."*

–Alan Sherry

her old friend Ruby Crawford, another Golden Spur resident, and asked Crawford to take her parents to Golden Spur's storm shelter. Crawford agreed. When Spencer double-checked about 6 p.m., no one answered the telephone. She was relieved; Crawford and her parents must be safe in the shelter.

Across Andover, people were stepping into their yards, looking out their windows to see if the tornado warnings were true.

At the edge of town, Alan Sherry also was watching the skies. A detective with the Andover Police Department, Sherry finally saw what he was looking for: a tornado, south and west of McConnell Air Force Base. "It was almost white," Sherry says.

He alerted dispatchers. Dispatchers passed the word on police radios. In the center of Andover, city officials ordered the sounding of the city's warning siren and a dispatcher pressed the siren's radio control trigger. Nothing happened. The dispatcher pressed again, and again nothing happened. The trigger was pressed four times, but the siren never sounded.

Police and fire units were quickly dispatched to circulate through the streets, sounding the sirens on their vehicles to warn residents of the danger.

The growing, gyrating tornado blackened as it consumed trees, roofs and cars southwest of Andover. "It kept getting larger and larger," Sherry says.

Andover Police Sgt. Paul Troy See was in his patrol car, heading to Golden Spur when he heard about Sherry's sighting. Although See lived in the park, he wasn't worried about his wife Roseanna and family. He had already telephoned her three times to make sure she

and their three children went to the storm shelter in the municipal building. Roseanna, her children and some friends left their mobile home at 6:10.

As See entered Golden Spur, he knew that the city's storm sirens hadn't gone off. He cruised the roads among the mobile homes to warn his neighbors. A few drops of rain spattered his windshield as he drove with sirens sounding and lights flashing. He made no announcements.

"I guess I could have," See says. But his sweep through the park should have stood out as extraordinary, he says.

The park looked nearly deserted, although See wasn't looking around much. His eyes were trained to the west where the now-black funnel loomed close on the horizon. He was trying to gauge how much longer he could warn people before seeking shelter himself.

"To be honest, I was watching the tornado to see how I was doing," See says. "I could see it really clearly as I turned back to the west."

As he continued to drive through the park, a few people walked. A vehicle or two rushed in or out of driveways.

Karen McCrary, raced her car into the entrance to Golden Spur where she lived. She had been having a soft drink with her daughter, Sarah, 4, at Carol's Kitchen, a restaurant in the Andover Square shopping center, a half-mile north of Golden Spur, when she first heard the warning. She was waiting for her husband, Tony McCrary, to get off work at the Four-Star Video store in the shopping center when her ex-husband, Don Morrison, ran into the restaurant, acting as a one-man

Left: The tornado strikes the Golden Spur Mobile Home Park. At this point, the funnel's winds were swirling at about 300 miles per hour.

Andover Police Sgt. Paul Troy See's squad-car camera recorded the last minute before the tornado struck Andover.

warning force.

"He's a guy who doesn't panic, and the guy was panicking. He said, 'Get the hell out of here, get out!'"McCrary says.

She and her daughter ran to her car. McCrary started it and floored the accelerator. "We hit 80 coming out of the parking lot," she says.

To her right as she drove south on Andover Road, McCrary saw the malignant cloud, "big, black and ugly."

Her daughter cried, "Hurry up, Mommy, hurry up! We're not going to make it!"

Fire trucks circulated through town, sounding their sirens and urging people to take shelter. One turned into the parking lot at Pizza Hut, next door to Livingston's restaurant. Charlene Fairman, a waitress at Livingston's, heard the firefighter's announcement: "Run for your life! Get out!"

"The fear in that man's voice, I will never forget," Fairman says.

She ran. She and about a dozen others from Livingston's hurried to the basement in Pizza Hut, following a longstanding arrangement between the managers of the two businesses.

As Fairman and others from the restaurants waited anxiously in the basement of Pizza Hut, a dark-gray, almost black, cloud loomed over the people who were still outdoors. The cloud was silhouetted against a lighter gray sky, dipped ominously to the ground, rolling forward as if it were a slow-moving wall.

In the Countryside Third Addition, Janet Kiser, 40, was unaware of the danger until minutes before the tornado struck. Kiser, thin and blond and quick to laugh at her

predicament, was home in her nightgown and robe, recuperating from surgery the previous week. Her husband and children left the house, on their way to a church youth party.

"They all walked out then they all walked back in," says Kiser, a homemaker. Her husband, Kelly Kiser, a statistician at Boeing, told her that he saw a tornado on the horizon. He did not think it would ever get to their house, but he said, "I think we all ought to go downstairs."

The children Katy, 12, and Kyle, 15, protested that Mom wasn't supposed to go up and down stairs while she was healing, but the parents assured them that it was OK to make an exception. The family had lived in the house for only 10 months. It was their first home with a basement.

Others were also unaware of the danger. About three blocks away on the northern edge of the neighborhood, Steve Rockstad, and his wife Patricia, were in the basement of their rented duplex, watching a videotape on television. They had no idea how grave the weather had become.

Then the telephone rang. When the Rockstads shut off the tape to answer the phone, the television reverted to a local channel and for the first time they heard the news that a tornado was heading toward their house. On the telephone, their 19-year-old son Shad asked what he should do if he confronted hail on his way home from work in Wichita. As the call ended, the Rockstads heard police sirens. Steve looked out the front window to check the sky.

"It looked real passive," he says. But when he

*"Run for your life! Get out!"*
–An Andover Firefighter

A pile of debris marked the site of Livingston's Restaurant. Waitress Charlene Fairman, other restaurant employees and customers survived by taking shelter in the basement of the neighboring Pizza Hut. Photo by Tom Schoening.

Right: The tornado demolished Tollie Hartmann's garage but left her cars. Hartmann took this photo the day after the tornado.

*"I couldn't see it coming. It looked too big to be a tornado. It looked like a massive cloud."*

–Tollie Hartmann

looked through the sliding glass doors at the rear of the house, Steve saw the funnel coming across the golf course. Half joking, he asked his wife if she wanted to see a tornado.

The funnel they were looking at would later be classified as an F5 tornado, "incredible tornado, incredible damage," according to meteorologists. At that moment, the tornado's winds were circulating at between 261 and 318 miles per hour.

The Rockstads called to their daughter, Angie, 14, to take cover with them in the basement. She had been playing in her room with a friend who lived nearby. The friend ran outside to go home. Angie yelled at him to come back, but the growing wind obscured her words. The dog, Harley, shoved her downstairs toward the basement.

The three Rockstads gathered in the basement bathroom to await the tornado. They heard footsteps. The bathroom door opened. Angie's friend ran inside.

Tollie Hartmann at first didn't believe she was seeing a tornado across the golf course behind her house.

"I could see it coming," she says. "It looked too big to be a tornado. It looked like a massive cloud."

She thought the tornado must be someplace else. But as it got closer, the debris flying in front of it convinced Hartmann to change her mind. She went to the basement of her home.

The intersection of Central Avenue and Andover Road is the commercial and physical center of the city with shopping centers on two corners. To the north of that intersection on Andover Road are the school and municipal buildings. The Kansas Turnpike angles across

the top third of the city.

In the mile south of the intersection of Central and Andover are commercial properties and two churches. Flanking Andover Road are the Countryside Third Addition housing development on the west and the Golden Spur Mobile Home Park on the east.

The tornado entered Andover on its western edge, first crossing into Butler County at the Green Valley Greens municipal golf course.

About 6:32 p.m., the tornado ripped the awning off the front of the Green Valley Greens clubhouse and dashed it through the front windows. The twister continued north and a little east through the golf course across the eighth and second fairways, shredding some trees, uprooting others, tossing concrete-and-wood benches about and scattering pull-carts in a ditch.

By now, Sgt. See was racing his squad car north on Andover Road to safety in the police station. He debated going through the mobile home park again before deciding to seek shelter.

"If I had made another pass I probably couldn't have made it out," he says. He could feel the air pressure dropping.

The car's engine roared as he accelerated north on Andover Road, but he turned off the car's siren and flashing lights. He waited for the traffic light to turn green at Andover and Central. He didn't want anyone to risk his or her life by stopping for a police car.

The twister headed due east from the golf course and entered Countryside Third Addition. Roaring, circulating winds rent and shattered scores of houses as their occupants shuddered in basements below. The tornado's

Bits of insulation were jammed into the metal fence that protects the entrance to the storm shelter on the Golden Spur Mobile Home Park. Between 200 and 300 people huddled in the shelter during the tornado. Photo by Tom Schoening.

path grew wider as it traveled, eventually reaching about 2,000 feet across.

As it tracked through the neighborhood, the tornado flung down another vortex that tore the wood-and-metal awning over the sidewalk at the Andover Square shopping center. It demolished shops on the east end of the center, including Carol's Kitchen. The winds crumpled a convenience store on the same corner as the shopping center and crushed a garage across from it on Central. Windows shattered. Roofs came apart.

Just north of there, off-duty Wesley Medical Center Lifewatch paramedic Dan Sharshel and Bill Barnes, night supervisor for Sedgwick County Emergency Medical Services, were surprised to find themselves nearly caught by the vortex.

A few minutes earlier, they had been setting up equipment for a "lift-a-thon" fund-raiser at Andover High School and they had driven to Sharshel's house north of Central to pick up an item they needed for the event. As they got to Andover Road en route to the school farther north of the intersection, they saw a funnel heading right for them. Later, they were to learn that it was the second vortex that had splintered off from the main funnel.

Winds lifted the rear of their van again and again as they sped away from the twister.

About three blocks south on Andover Road, Charlene Fairman fretted in the basement of the Pizza Hut. She knew Her husband and son, Jim and Jimmy Fairman, were driving back from an errand in Wichita. She wondered if they were safe.

At that moment Jim and Jimmy were just west of the intersection of Central and Andover. Their car was heading toward the twister as it sheared away the buildings on the west side of the intersection.

"Bricks were flying," Jim says. "The Coastal Mart was there, and then all of a sudden it wasn't. All you could see was the black cloud."

Jim stomped on the brakes, and the tornado moved across the road and headed away from them.

In the Countryside Third Addition, the winds launched balls, bicycles, barbecue grills, anything that wasn't fastened down. The things that were anchored shuddered before yielding, and then flew away.

Next to the golf course, Tollie Hartmann was in the basement talking on the phone to her stepson as the tornado passed by. She told him, "It's over me right now because my ears are popping."

She heard crashes and thuds. She heard her big, long trestle table hitting a wall, and she heard the storm's roar.

"It sounds like the B1 (bomber)," Hartmann said. "It was a definite, constant sound. It was just there. It didn't build to a crescendo and recede. It was just there."

Swirling around the tornado's center were chunks of insulation, siding, shingles and the millions of items that made up people's lives. From afar, the particles looked like chimney swifts preparing to settle for the night.

A block away under the stairs in the Mendoza basement, the Long and Mendoza families were on the floor, kneeling and praying. The members took turns praying, and it was Kathleen Long's turn while the twister hit. "I think that helped me not hear the noise," she says. Still, she was aware that above her were the sounds of the house breaking apart.

A couple blocks away at the Rockstads', Steve

*"Bricks were flying. The Coastal Mart was there, and then all of a sudden it wasn't. All you could see was the black cloud."*

– Jim Fairman

Less than 24 hours after the tornado struck, the Golden Spur Mobile Home Park is a twisted landscape, filled with debris. Photo by Bill Pfaff.

Right: A man climbs through the wreckage of the Golden Spur Mobile Home Park. Photo by Tom Schoening

*"We were packed in there like sardines."*

–Karen McCrary

realized that he had left his wallet upstairs, and he ran up to retrieve it.

"I looked out the front window, and there was debris circulating," he says. Steve remembered someone telling him once that if you see debris circulating, the tornado is above you.

He scurried back to the basement bathroom. He crouched on the floor and covered his head, not knowing whether a board would come crashing through the door at any moment.

"The lights went out, and you could hear all this wrenching noise and pounding," Steve says. Sounds of the storm echoed eerily in the room through the clothes-dryer vent.

Angie feared that they all might die, but her father was in awe. Steve commented on the air pressure, saying "This feels really weird." His ears were popping as they would in a pressurized airplane cabin.

As the tornado pummeled the house above, Steve tried to open the bathroom door, but the drastic drop in air pressure created a near-vacuum, and he couldn't.

The tornado rumbled across Andover Road and into Golden Spur.

In the middle of Golden Spur is a bunker that serves as the tornado shelter for the residents. As the tornado approached, neighbors — maybe 200, maybe 300 — crowded into the close space.

Arched corrugated steel and chain-link fencing mark the entrance to the shelter. Inside, it's 44 paces to the back. Five paces across. Six and a half feet from the floor to the slightly arching reinforced concrete ceiling. Two-by-12 boards atop concrete blocks line each wall,

forming two long benches. A third bench runs down the center. This was not comfort, but it was safety.

"We were packed in there like sardines," says Karen McCrary, who made it to the shelter with her daughter a minute before the tornado reached it. Her husband, Tony, clambered in about 45 seconds after her. He too, had raced his car to the spot.

Screams and moans filled the air in the shelter as the tornado bore down at 6:40 p.m. The lights went out, and only sound existed: the roar of the tornado, the screech and groan of grinding steel and aluminum, the terrified wails of the people.

"It sounded like a metal grinder, and I guess it was. Loud, real loud," Karen McCrary says.

Not everyone in the park made it to the shelter. Some were unconcerned. Some were unaware of the storm or acted too late. And no one knows why others didn't make it. For 11 people in the park, hesitation spelled death. Scores of others suffered severe injuries.

One of them was Allen Sargent, a structural draftsman at Boeing Aircraft Co. He was having dinner with his wife of nine months, Katherine, her daughter, Kristina Kinyon, 13, and his daughter Michelle Sargent, 25, when they heard the tornado warning on television. They checked the weather, but all seemed OK. No one saw a funnel or heard a siren.

Moments later, Allen and Michelle looked up and through a window saw the twister coming at them. He ordered the girls to lie in the bathtub, and he and his wife went to the bedroom, where he told Katherine to get down and put a pillow over her head.

The back windows blew out before Allen Sargent

could get on the floor. His home moaned under the twister's assault. The trailer turned on its side, stood on end and started coming apart. Walls, roof, windows burst. Sargent clung to his wife, then he blacked out.

Elsewhere in the park, Robert Meininger, was trying to get to the shelter. His daughter, son-in-law and their three children had come to have dinner with him that evening. Meininger, a glazier, took them to the shelter, then went back to lock his trailer; he had lost all his belongings in a fire in 1977 and couldn't bear to lose everything again. He told his daughter, Teresa Warren, that he would return.

Betty Sanders, was home alone in Golden Spur when a neighbor, Wanda Walker, called to warn her of the approaching tornado. Walker went to help Sanders, but she didn't make it in time.

Elsie and Anton Kemper were watching "M*A*S*H" on television when Anton spotted the twister. The couple ran to a storage shed near their trailer, and he held tightly to his wife. But the winds swept her away.

Denise Peterson, a veterinarian's assistant, was home in Golden Spur, too. Her boss had warned her of the storm before she left work at Gary Dale Harmon's veterinary clinic. But she didn't make it to the shelter. No one knows why.

Nor is anyone certain why Bessie Temple didn't go. Or Robert and Gladys Manes, or their friend Ruby Crawford, or her friend Joe Bobbitt. Those who knew Crawford, manager of the Andover Senior Citizens Center, felt sure she died helping, like the elderly Manses, just as Mary Lou Spencer had asked Crawford to do.

Nearby, the Kanavy family, Ronald I, Ronald II and Pat of Wichita were in their car on their way to visit friends in Andover when they met the tornado. They stopped the car and ran for a ditch. Pat, lay on the bottom. Her husband, Ronald I covered her body with his own, and their son lay beside them. Only Pat would survive.

As for Joe Marks, who had eaten dinner earlier at Livingston's, he stayed in his trailer, as he always did, to ride out the storm. The tornado rumbled away from Golden Spur.

The storm had already been on the ground for almost 20 miles, but it wasn't finished. Its winds slowed to 158 to 260 miles per hour, ranking it as merely a "severe" or "devastating" tornado rather than an incredible one. That means the tornado left a few things standing.

The tornado turned northward, taking out a collection of houses adjacent to Golden Spur, then headed northeast, parallel to the Kansas Turnpike.

About two miles northeast of Andover near 13th Street and 162 Street north, Brook Ibarra, was eating dinner with her mother, brother, her 10-month-old daughter and a friend. They heard a tornado had hit Haysville but couldn't imagine it would last long enough to reach them. Then they heard it was going through Andover.

They left their seats and looked out the door. They saw debris shoot into the air as the tornado struck the trailer park about two miles away. The five ran to Ibarra's car and got in to drive the half-mile to a neighbor's house, which had a basement. But they were too late.

"Another 20 seconds and we would have been in her basement," says Ibarra's mother, Sharon Williamson.

*"Another 20 seconds and we would have been in her basement."*

–Sharon Williamson

35

Metal tangled around a tree is all that survived of one trailer in the Golden Spur Mobile Home Park. Photo by Brett Bohannon.

Right: Rhondda Street in Golden Spur Mobile Home Park is visible in the foreground of this photo. Photo by Richard Parks.

*"I remember seeing sheet metal, bricks, trees and a cow flying by."*

–Brook Ibarra

Debris was falling out of the air as they drove. They decided to try to leave the car. The first four out of the car filled a nearby depression in the ground.

The baby, Taylor, was on the bottom. The friend, Charisma Waddill, 19, covered Taylor with her body. Williamson got on top of Waddill, and her son Jeff Williamson was next.

Ibarra got in a ditch a few yards away and grabbed a small pine tree.

"I remember seeing sheet metal, bricks, trees and a cow flying by," Ibarra says.

Then Ibarra, too, was flying. She cleared a 4-foot barbed wire fence. The gale dragged her across the ground, lifted, carried, dropped, dragged and lifted her again.

"I was doing somersaults and just being thrown around, and the whole time I could hear my baby crying," Ibarra says. "I felt my collarbone break, and my lung collapse. I knew I was going to die and I was yelling, 'God, take me now!' I just wanted to get it over with."

She went up and down three times, and at last landed next to a piece of wood the tornado had jammed into the ground. "I just grabbed onto it and held on," she says.

Her mother, horrified at seeing her daughter swept away, worried too for herself. She and Jeff in unison began reciting the Lord's Prayer.

The tornado continued northeast. It angled closer to the Turnpike where alarmed motorists were seeking shelter.

Among them were Lee Mann and Jack Hughes of Jefferson County, about 150 miles away. They were driving toward Wichita when they ran into hail and saw the funnel coming. It was hitting Andover when they first saw it. "It was black as could be," Mann says.

They pulled their pickup truck off under an overpass about one mile northeast of the Andover exit.

"It was almost as if we were a bull's eye or an 'X' on a map," Mann says. "It was coming straight toward the bridge."

Other cars were stopping, too, and Hughes was directing people to take cover under the bridge's girders. For a while he watched the storm, which appeared to move slowly. Then he joined the half-dozen travelers under the girders. Everyone curled into fetal positions. A roar, as if from nearby jet engines, drowned out all other sounds.

"Then, there was total stillness before it hit again," Mann says. "You could still hear the roar, but there was no air movement. there was no wind. There was no rain. There was absolutely nothing just prior to its hitting us.

"Jack raised up and said we were safe, it's passed us. Then this other force hit us from the other side, and it was a much stronger force than the first."

Mann was praying out loud. "I think I prayed to about four religions," she says.

She thought they were going to be electrocuted, and lightning appeared to be everywhere around them. Later Mann would learn that huge towers carrying high-tension electrical power lines were damaged as the storm rumbled through.

"I was hugging my purse under me," Mann says. "I wanted them to be able to identify my body. I thought this was it. There is no escaping."

Amid the roar, she saw objects circulating around the twister.

"I guess it was trailer parts, parts of houses," Mann says.

The pieces were large and easily identifiable. Flecks of pink insulation stood out for their unnatural color. "It was almost mesmerizing," Mann says.

The tornado continued to the northeast. It snatched a home here and there in the countryside, tossing animals to their deaths and scattering livestock. It ripped up trees, crumpled cars and the outbuildings of farms, and still kept moving.

Gereda Edwards, 67, whose home was near Towanda, saw the storm coming, and a neighbor appeared seeking shelter. The two of them climbed into a crawl space under Edwards' home, her retirement home. It was the home she had finally just finished to her satisfaction.

"It sounded like an airplane crashed into the side of the house," Edwards says. "Boards were ripping and tearing loose."

Then she heard a bigger roar amid the steady roar of the winds. She is sure that was when the carpet pulled away from the floor just above them.

"It kind of quieted down and then dust from the east came pouring up and under the house, covering us up with dirt and sand," she says. "Then it quieted again, and the garage left. I could see daylight, and insulation started blowing on us from the northwest. Then it was all over, quiet."

The twister continued to the northeast. Its winds slowed to the F1 or F2 level of 73 to 157 miles per hour.

The tornado entered oil fields west-northwest of El Dorado, sending a few oil tanks rolling across the countryside.

For a few more miles the tornado haphazardly damaged whatever lay in its path until, at last spent, it disappeared about five miles north of El Dorado.

After the roar was silence, utter silence. "All that noise, and then there was nothing," Janet Kiser says.

Perhaps the contrast between abrupt violence and false tranquility heightened the impression, but it was a strong one. Even for Tony McCrary inside the Golden Spur shelter, amid a panic-stricken and claustrophobic crowd.

"After it passed, people were still screaming," he says. But their moans and gasps seemed to be in the background somehow. "Otherwise, it was almost total silence," McCrary says.

People in the subdivision west of Andover Road and in the shelter in the park, people in basements and culverts and ditches and crawl spaces began climbing into the daylight. For a moment, most people underscored the quiet with their own silence. The scene before them was unspeakably horrible, too unbelievable.

For before them lay nothingness, or as much of nothing as hundreds of former homes could have been.

Only an occasional, twisted tree interrupted the view across acres and acres of flatlands. No street signs, no special tree, no parked cars distinguished one spot on the terrain from another.

Later, when they tried to describe the scene, the

Across from 209 W. Douglas in Andover, the scene is desolate on the day after the tornado. Photo by Janet Kiser.

Right: Humor amid sadness at the site of the Storrer Home. The sign reads, "Garage Sale." Photo by Lynn and Neil Ziegler.

*"I just want to say one thing. The four of us are still alive, and that's all that matters. What you see out there doesn't matter. "*

–Kelly Kiser

people would grope for the right words. It looked like a bomb had gone off, but there was no smoke or fire. It looked like a salvage yard, but the items were too disorganized even for such a place. It looked, in short, like nothing they had ever seen before, because none had seen the ruin caused by so intense a tornado.

Smashed cars were stacked with shingles. Lumber and clothes shared a spot. The only constants were dirt and bits of pink fiberglass insulation, which seemed to cling to everything. Twisted pieces of metal — mobile home siding, mostly — hugged the occasional surviving pole or crushed tree.

In the Countryside Third Addition, half of Tollie Hartmann's home was left. She walked up the basement stairs, saw light shining through the roof and saw debris. "I had walls where I had stairs," she says.

Then she looked east across the street and saw rubble where houses had been just minutes ago.

"All the houses around were leveled. There wasn't much, there just wasn't much." Hartmann's house was the only one for blocks that was still standing.

People began to take stock of each other. "The first reaction was to account for everyone you could account for," says Hartmann, who was not hurt. "Everybody was counting everybody else."

At the Kiser home, the family waited a minute in the basement bathroom before Kelly Kiser announced he would go check on things and return.

He walked out in the basement, and the rest of the family saw trash littering the floor. They looked up and saw there was no ceiling.

"The trash and glass were just everywhere," Janet

Kiser says.

Kelly came right back into the bathroom and shut the door behind him.

"I just want to say one thing," he said. "The four of us are still alive, and that's all that matters. What you see out there doesn't matter. Now, when we go upstairs, there's not going to be a roof on our house, but remember that doesn't matter."

The children said, "Oh, look at my window" and pointed to other broken and missing belongings. Kelly kept saying, "We can fix these things."

Once outside, the Kiser family looked east. "We could see the whole trailer park," Janet says. "There was nothing... All those homes were leveled. No dogs barking. No birds flying around. I kept thinking I'm not (really) here."

At the Mendoza basement, the Mendozas and Longs got to their feet and looked up the stairs. Kathleen Long said to Kathy Mendoza, "Oh Kathy, let me see what your house is like."

Long went upstairs and returned quickly. "Oh, it's bad, it's bad," she said. "We'd better get out of here."

They climbed out and walked toward Faith Baptist Church on Central. As they walked, they found Beverly Long's purse. When they reached the church, they called Kathy Mendoza's mother in Independence, Kan., and asked her to notify relatives that the Long family was all right. Their telephone calls were among the last to get out before people overloaded the lines.

Suzie Storrer was in a panic. Storrer, a teacher, had been at a National Education Association executive board meeting at a restaurant in Wichita when she heard

The metal ribbon in the center of the photo is the remnant of a trailer frame in the Golden Spur Mobile Home Park. Three wheels are visible at the top of the arch of metal. Photo by Bill Pfaff.

sirens go off. She knew her two daughters, Misty, 14, and Kelsey, 11, were home alone in the Countryside Third Addition. Storrer is originally from Emporia where a tornado in 1974 devastated part of town. "I respect sirens," she says.

Storrer asked a waitress about the storm, and learned that a tornado had been spotted at Greenwich and Harry roads.

"That's too close for comfort," she declared. Storrer left the meeting and sped east toward home, driving 85 and 90 miles per hour.

"But I stopped at every stop sign and stop light," she says. "If I had left any earlier, I would have been in it."

Debris covered the roadway, and she had to stop the car four blocks from her house. Storrer tried in vain to find out whether the tornado had reached her street.

"Finally, I couldn't take it any more," she says.

Storrer, who race walks, removed her high-heeled shoes and sprinted barefoot through the glass and debris to find her children.

"Yes, you do wet your pants when you're that scared, but there were no cuts on my feet, although my hose were shredded," Storrer says. "I yelled their names, and then I said, 'Where is our house?' You lose perspective when everything is flattened."

At last she found her daughters, standing unharmed in a neighbor's driveway.

"I had $200,000 of antiques uninsured, but my kids were alive, and that's what matters," she says.

All that remained of her house were strips of carpet tacks and linoleum in the kitchen, and the basement.

Storrer learned that the girls had been in the basement when the Sedgwick County tornado warning was called. But they went upstairs to get a pizza that was being delivered to them. They lingered to look for a rainbow. A television announcer had said that a stunning rainbow was visible. Instead of a rainbow, the girls saw the tornado. The girls ran to the basement. They never heard what happened to the woman who delivered their pizza.

Storrer had seen the destruction of tornadoes before. She had helped clean up after the Emporia tornado, but she couldn't believe the destruction she saw at her own home. People from Hesston later told her the Andover tornado was 10 times worse than the one that ripped their town apart in 1990.

"I had nothing, nothing furniture-wise on the first floor," Storrer says. "Before, the furnishings had included 25 antique sink cabinets.

"Now I don't have any. I don't even have pieces. My husband had Aladdin lamps, 40 of them, and he had one, a glass one, left."

In that neighborhood, all the residents was essentially OK, although it would take hours for everyone to be sure. The adjacent Catholic church, however, was gone.

Detective Sherry, whose patrol car had been spun around twice by the twister, set up an initial disaster command post at the neighborhood's northwest corner.

Electricity and telephone service were out, although in the housing development those lines are buried. People soon heard and smelled natural gas hissing from broken lines. Freon spewing from broken air conditioners added to the sound.

Sherry called the utility companies from the cellular

Charlene and Jimmy Fairman stand in front of the wreckage that was once their home in the Golden Spur Mobile Home Park. The sofa was dug out of the debris. Photo by Jim Fairman.

A broken bicycle is among the debris in the Golden Spur Mobile Home Park on the morning after the tornado. Photo by LuVerne Paine.

Right: Rescuers pull wreckage off the body of Robert Meininger, which was discovered by his wife and daughter the day after the tornado. Photo by Gary Bearden.

*"We could see the total destruction in the trailer park"*

–Tony McCrary

phone in his car as the police dispatcher radioed the telephone numbers to him. It would be many hours before the day he started at 8 a.m. would end.

Others were emerging from the police station north of the tornado's path, and the radios squawked orders for Emergency Medical Service and warned of downed power lines.

Jimmy Fairman, 12, bolted from his father's car on Central Avenue. Ignoring the fallen electrical wires, the boy ran toward the place where Livingston's restaurant had been and cried out for his mother, Charlene Fairman. Jimmy could see that Livingston's, where she had been working was gone. He was sure she was dead. "We found Mom sitting on rubble," Jimmy says.

Across Andover Road at Golden Spur, the roll call brought grim results.

The first thing Tony and Karen McCrary saw upon emerging from the shelter was Karen's car, a recent present from Tony. The car was upside down in a swimming pool.

They looked and stepped carefully. Power lines weren't buried in the park and they sparked and fizzled before the dazed residents. Tony says he just wanted to move slowly and cautiously through the debris to safety. His home was one of the few identifiable in Golden Spur.

"We could see the total destruction in the trailer park," he says. "I could see that our trailer was still standing, but it had been lifted off the frame and set back down."

All around, gas hissed, water shot into the air and electrical lines spat while people moaned and cried in despair.

"We were afraid to go, afraid to stay," Karen says.

The Fairmens by now had all been reunited. Jim and Jimmy set out across Andover Road to try to help their neighbors in Golden Spur.

"You could hear the people yelling, but you couldn't do anything," the boy says.

His father says, "I kept saying, we got to help these people! We were doing what we could, but there was nothing we could accomplish."

Jim and Jimmy found the bodies of Ronald Kanavy I and Ronald Kanavy II as well as their injured wife and mother, Pat. They found the mangled body of their neighbor Joe Marks. They found a woman, semi-conscious.

Dan Sharshel and Bill Barnes, the off-duty emergency medical technicians, found an ambulance that had just arrived at Andover Square Shopping Center from an undamaged part of town. Sharshal and Barnes still didn't know they had seen only a splinter funnel. The real damage lay about four blocks away from where they were standing.

The ambulance supervisor, recognizing them, asked them to go to Golden Spur and warned of reports of up to 30 fatalities. Sharshel and Barnes contacted Lifewatch and other agencies by radio to seek assistance before setting out.

With only their rubber gloves to identify them as rescuers, they nonetheless attracted a following of residents eager to help. Sharshel and Barnes directed them to find doors, boards or anything else that might be used as stretchers.

The first two people they found were dead. Then they

# The Tornadoes of 1991

## For a time,

it seemed as if the 26th of every month brought disaster to some corner of Kansas. On March 26, tornadoes roared through Pratt and Reno counties, causing injuries and damaging property. On April 26, the most devastating tornadoes of the year struck the cities of Andover, Wichita, Haysville and roared through many counties, including Cowley, Elk, Atchison, and Jefferson. Twenty people died and hundreds were injured. But as the storm season continued it became clear that practically every day of the 1991 storm season in Kansas was going to be dangerous. By August, the National Weather Service had recorded 115 Kansas tornadoes–more than any other year since the Weather Service began keeping track. Most of the tornadoes occurred from March to June.

## March
(Shown in Blue)–Among the reports of March tornadoes were four in Pratt and Reno counties and lone tornadoes in Allen, Sumner, Cowley, Douglas, Shawnee, Chase, and Marion counties. Hardest hit were the towns of Abbyville and Willowbrook.

## April
(Shown in Red)–The most dangerous month of the year brought tornadoes to about 20 counties. Along with the tornadoes already mentioned, funnels touched down in the counties of Washington, Wabaunsee, Cloud, Greenwood, Woodson, Montgomery, Labette, Sumner, Harper, Chase and Morris. The largest number of tornadoes was reported on April 26 while serious outbreaks were also seen on April 11 and 12..

## May
(Shown in Green)–Tornadoes rumbled throughout Kansas in May, including May 15 and 16 when funnel after funnel touched down in Finney and Sherman counties in western Kansas. May 16 also brought a tornado to southern Sedgwick County that came close to matching the path taken by the fatal April 26 tornado.

## June
(shown in Yellow)– Tornado activity lessened but did not disappear as summer appeared. Funnels touched down in Sherman, Douglas and Butler counties.

---

### Fujita Tornado Scale

Each tornado on the map is marked with its intensity rating from the Fujita Tornado Intensity Scale. Developed by Dr. Theodore Fujita from the University of Chicago, this scale assigns an "F" number to each tornado to rate the storm's damaging power. Depending on the intensity of the tornado, the wind inside a funnel can be swirling at speeds ranging from 40 miles per hour to 318 miles per hour.

  F0,    40-72 miles per hour
  F1,   73-112 miles per hour
  F2, 113-157 miles per hour
  F3, 158-206 miles per hour
  F4, 207-260 miles per hour
  F5, 261-318 miles per hour

A June 1991 thunderstorm sends forks of lightning onto downtown Wichita. Photo by Audie Thornburg.

Meteorologists say that every severe thunderstorm has the potential for disaster in the form of tornadoes, high winds, floods and dangerous lightning.

Right: Cars and fragments of buildings are piled against the remains of a tree on Wilson Road near Willowbrook. Photo by Sandra Watts.

Clouds tower in a glowing golden sky after an April rain shower near the town of Douglas. Photo by Audie Thornburg.

A tornado builds in intensity on May 16 as it moves past Kenneth and June Sparr's wheat field 4 miles south of Clearwater. Photo by June Sparr.

Four days after one April 26 tornado tore through Cowley County, bent trunks and jagged branches are all that remain of these trees 4 1/2 miles east of Winfield on Highway 160. Photo by Mary Ann Drum.

Only a few homes survived with anything intact after the tornado rolled through the Golden Spur Mobile Home Park in Andover. At the center of the photo, a metal frame, complete with three pairs of wheels, is the only remaining part of one mobile home. Photo by Sandra Watts.

Harold Kruse and his grandson Eric Lovig watch fire consume the last of the Kruse barn north of Hanover. The rest of the barn was damaged by a tornado. Photo by Dean Lovig.

**Right:** In June a Cabbage Patch doll remains stranded in a tree 1/4 mile east of the intersection of Andover Road and Central not far from where the tornado destroyed the Golden Spur Mobile Home Park. Photo by Marganne Winter Oxley.

The tip of the long white tornado is obsured by a cloud of dirt minutes before the tornado destroys Rudy Beck's farm house near Clearwater on May 16. June Sparr took this photo looking over her wheat field toward Beck's home, which is to the left of the funnel.

Right: Strips of lath are all that remain of the front bedroom on George and Mildred Benson's home near Hutchinson. The tornado consumed plaster, windows, roof and furniture. Photo by A. Benson.

Below: An upside-down car tops a pile of wreckage at George and Milded Benson's home. Photo by Sandra Watts.

Right: Photographer Jon Davis took this photo on May 16 when the tornado was 1 mile away from him and 3 miles west southwest of Clearwater.

The wreckage of Jack and Chelsea McCreery's farm near Clearwater is clear in this photo looking out through the chaos of their living room. Photo by Colleen Heitman.

The wad of metal that used to be a shop is visible in this photo taken out of Mildred and George Benson's northwest bedroom. Photo by A Benson.

The home of Peter and Nadine Kraft in Wichita has been opened to the sky by the tornado. Photo by Charlene Watleg.

The tornado knocked over tombstones in Pleasant Valley Cemetery 6 miles south of Winfield. Photo by Mary Ann Drum.

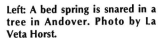

Above: Rumors are as abundant after a tornado as debris. In this case, people claimed that a snake had been driven through a tree by the force of the tornado. No evidence of such a luckless reptile was ever found, but this photo shows the body of a snake that was apparently killed when it curled up inside a tree and the tree broke in the wind. Someone tried to pull the snake out of the hole in the tree. Photo by Jane Laughlin.

Left: A house plant provides the only touch of green in the devastated landcape of Barbara Pearce's home in Wichita. Photo by Judy Pearce.

Above: A funnel touches down at El Dorado Lake on May 16. Photo by Charles Brewer.

Above: Friends help clean up the remains of a home near Kansas Highway 4 northeast of Topeka. Photo by Gloria Harrington.

A tornado threatens Willow-brook on the west edge of Hutchinson. Photo by Sandra Watts.

Top: Will Winter Oxley, 5, stands next to a car that was blown off the turnpike near Andover and wrapped around a tree. The car fell to the ground the day after the tornado. Photo by John Winter.

Bottom: The southwest corner of Ray Macheda and Lance Darling's house in Wichita is still standing–sort of. Photo by Brad Hoover.

**Right:** A rainbow appears as the tornado rolls toward McConnell Air Force Base after thundering through Haysville and Wichita. Photo by Grag Mullins.

**Right:** A pile of Kasey Werner's newly cleaned toys dries on the lawn of his Wichita home the day after the tornado. Kasey, the son of Donald Thomas, searched for his toys, discovered them covered with mud, put them in a bucket and washed them off. Photo by Derrick Vogt.

**Above:** Only the greenhouse frames remain, sagging over the flowers of Meyer's Garden Spot Nursery and Greenhouse in Wichita. Photo by Gloria Hardesty.

**Above:** The remnants of Robert Dolan's house near Paxico are scattered among twisted trees and damged vehicles. Photo by Robert Mabranahan.

Right: Brad Wilt talks while his wife Penny holds the telephone, which survived the tornado despite the fact the Wilt's home did not. Behind them volunteers work on their home in Abbyville. Photo by Peggy Webb.

Left: A silver Christmas tree garland is tangled in the branches of a tree near Piedmont after one tornado. Photo by Buzz Shaddy.

One tornado near El Dorado pulled this fence of heavy pipe out of the ground, including the concrete that anchored each fence post. Photo by Doug Gunn.

Left: The staff and patients of the McConnell Air Force Base hospital survived even though the hospital did not. Notice the mangled cars to the right of center. Photo by Sgt. Victor Trisvan.

A tree on McConnell Air Force Base is riddled with debris, including a boot. Photo by Mike Hunsucker.

Left: A May 16 tornado rumbles toward Clearwater. The funnel missed the town by only one mile. Photo by Jon Davies.

Above: Photographer Larry W. Smith watched this cloud form a tornado behind his parent's house in El Dorado on May 27. The tornado dissipated after crossing a highway.

Above: Pieces of a car are tangled around a tree in a pasture 6 miles east of Winfield on Highway 160. Photo by Mary Ann Drum.

Right: The view inside the Non-Commissioned Officers Club at McConnell Air Force Base shows a wall decorated with insignia. Photo by Tim C. Sutton.

**Above: A tornado rolls through the countryside near Clearwater on May 16. Photo by June Sparr.**

**Right: A broken tree is visible through the hole left in the wall of this Cowley County home after the tornado tore away the chimney. Photo by John Decker.**

The people of Andover work to salvage their lives at 9:30 a.m. on the day after the tornado. Across the street from these homes is the Golden Spur Mobile Home Park. Photo by LuVerne Paine.

found Bessie Temple.

"One person thought they saw dirt moving. It was her breathing," Sharshel says. She told them her name, and volunteers carried her away from the wreckage on a door. She died later that evening.

Together, the two found three very seriously injured people in the next few minutes and five bodies all in just a half-block square area. After about a half-hour, Sharshel was called away to the intersection of Andover and Central to help a rescue helicopter land.

"People were running around under the helicopter; it was chaos," he says, but a Butler County firefighter group was roping the area off. Eventually, the helicopter made the first and only airlift rescue. Soon, winds rose, lightning threatened, and rain fell on the stricken area, making it unsafe for a helicopter to fly.

Back at Golden Spur, Allen Sargent was sitting 30 feet from the site of his trailer and wondering what had happened to his home, his family.

"There was nothing left," he says. "There was just bare dirt where the trailer was.

"The girls were gone, the trailer was gone. Kathy was gone."

Sargent didn't realize he had a spike up his foot, but he quickly learned he couldn't walk.

Soon, emergency workers stanched the bleeding and stabilized his condition — his right arm was injured, and he had a deep, 18-inch gash across his left buttock. He waited to be taken to the hospital. His daughter Michelle and stepdaughter Kristina were both seriously injured. Rescuers found them and sent them to the hospital.

As for Sargent's wife, he didn't find out until the next day that she was dead.

"Head trauma that killed her instantly," Sargent says, his voice breaking.

Also dead: Joe Bobbitt, whose chest was crushed; his friend Ruby Crawford and the Manses, whom she tried to save; Elsie Kemper, who'd been torn from her husband's grasp; Joe Marks, who thought he could ride out the storm; veterinarian aide Denise Peterson, whose safety may have been hampered by her hearing loss; and Betty Sanders, whose body was found against the wheels of a neighbor's trailer. Her would-be rescuer Wanda Walker survived. Robert Meininger was nowhere in sight. His body would not be discovered for 20 hours.

The injured of Golden Spur — the people who survived after being outdoors or in their mobile homes when the tornado struck — suffered every imaginable trauma injury. They had been pummeled with boards, sliced with steel, thrown against trees.

Some were able to walk to the triage area set up at Andover and Central. Some sat about, waiting their turn. Others were hurt too badly to sit.

"If you can imagine being thrown in a puddle of mud and having somebody beat on you with a ball bat for a few minutes, that's how everybody looked," paramedic Sharshel says.

He found one man whose injuries looked as though he had hit a wall. Indeed, lying nearby was a wall from a mobile home, and it bore an impression, an outline, of the man's figure.

Volunteers and emergency officials continued their search efforts into the early morning hours. Those with missing relatives frantically tried to find them. It would be hours before the family of Golden Spur resident Betty Parks would learn that she had gone to a house instead

*"If you can imagine being thrown in a puddle of mud for a few minutes and having somebody beat on you with a ball bat for a few minutes, that's how everybody looked."*

–Paramedic Dan Sharshel

Bits of metal hang in the barren branches of the trees in the Golden Spur Mobile Home Park as residents continue to look for their possessions on the third morning after the tornado. Photo by Rodger C.Bain.

Right: Rescuers work to free a pregnant woman who was caught in the tornado northwest of the Golden Spur Mobile Home Park. The woman survived, but the baby died. Photo by Tom Schoening.

*"It's like a giant vacuum sweeper sucked all this stuff up and decided to drop it."*

–Russ Griffith

of the church, and that she was safe.

Sgt. See ended up searching for survivors in the housing development.

"One of the first houses I went into, I went upstairs and saw a baby crib. I was scared to death I would find something," says See, father of three young children. Happily, the crib was empty and its usual occupant apparently safe.

Mary Lou Spencer tried to get to Golden Spur from her job in Wichita to check on her parents, her friend Crawford, and her home. Traffic was at a crawl as residents, would-be volunteers and sightseers jammed the roads from Wichita to Andover.

"I sat for two and a half hours because of traffic, within one-quarter mile of the county line," Spencer says. Once she made it to the county line, Spencer couldn't get through because of ambulances.

She wasn't too worried, though. Spencer was certain her parents had gone to the shelter and were safe. Spencer didn't make it to Golden Spur that night, but that evening she talked to her son who had made it to the trailer park. He said, "There's nothing there, Mother."

Spencer called a telephone number announced on television for people seeking relatives. Someone told her that Ruby Crawford had been seen going to the hospital and that the "elderly people" were there and they were all right. But a night of calling hospitals located no one. It wasn't until the next day that Spencer learned that Crawford and her parents had been killed.

Russ Griffith, the golf course pro, had headed to town after shutting down his operations. But, seeing the

funnel, he turned back west on Central and drove away from the storm's path. When the tornado passed, he circled back to the golf course. Griffith managed to call his wife and let her know he was safe. When he tried again later, he couldn't get through.

"I just proceeded to board up the windows and close the place up," he says. "I stayed here until around 10:30 guarding against vandals."

A goose sat out by a practice putting green. Little pieces of houses and furniture and cloth and bigger pieces of boards and shingles and asphalt and broken glass and tree limbs cluttered the area.

"It's like a giant vacuum sweeper sucked all this stuff up and decided to drop it," Griffith says.

In the fields outside of Andover, Brook Ibarra's mother, Sharon Williamson, was dazed. She put on the pair of glasses lying in front of her, but her own glasses were still on her face. The glasses she had picked up were from Jeff Williamson.

Ibarra had been blown a quarter-mile from her family and friends. From where she lay, Ibarra smelled smoke from downed power lines, and she saw the large engine from a John Deere tractor sitting 2 feet from her. Caked with mud, Ibarra stood up and began running and walking back to the place where her family and friends were just getting up. Ibarra's friend Waddill ran out to meet her and half-carried her the rest of the way.

Sharon Williamson was terrified. It seemed there was no way to help her daughter.

"It was obvious she was seriously hurt, her car was ruined, and I didn't know what we could do," Williamson says.

A few minutes later a truck carrying young men out chasing the tornado appeared. The group flagged the truck and the men called an ambulance on their citizens band radio.

Besides the injuries she immediately recognized, Ibarra also had a broken shoulder blade, broken vertebra in her neck and back, a severed nerve in one thumb. And lots of big bruises.

Sharon Williamson had torn ligaments and a cut from the hip to the back of her knee, "deep enough that when I put my hand back there to see what was wrong, my fingers went all the way in to the bone."

Jeff Williamson's leg was cut, and Waddill's leg was hurt. Little Taylor came through with just pock marks from the sand, mud and dirt.

The people under the Turnpike bridge northeast of Andover were very quiet for a moment once they were sure no more winds were coming.

They looked behind them and saw 20 or 30 people climb from a culvert down the road. "I didn't even know it was there," Lee Mann says.

Around her, people checked their vehicles under the bridge. Some windows and lights were broken, some contents were missing. An 18-wheeler lay on its side. Crumpled cars were strewn in a field. Sheet metal wrapped the median divider.

"There was debris, just stuff, everywhere," Mann says.

A hedge row of Osage orange trees looked like shredded toothpicks. The freshly waxed surface of Mann and Hughes' new truck was criss- crossed with grains of sand.

"You could see definitely the two directions of the wind," she says.

But the people were all right, except for being sandblasted. Mann's arm was raw for days.

Gereda Edwards was shaken as she emerged from the crawl space of her country home.

"I was just devastated," she says. "I couldn't believe it. I didn't have on any shoes, couldn't find any shoes. A big roll of tin was in the middle of the family room."

Although her purse lay at the door, her neighbor's car was gone. It had sailed about three-quarters miles away. Edwards' propane tank was found one and a half miles away. Her truck was a total loss. It was found resting on the spot where the propane tank had been.

"I started to try to find something that was good, see if there was anything I could find that was any good," she says.

Edwards wandered around a few minutes, and some people came up to see if she was all right. She asked a man to check on her son, who lives nearby.

"The man met my son coming to look for me," Edwards says.

Back in Andover, officials did their best to empty the area of people as the search-and-rescue operations continued and daylight failed. The medical people, meanwhile, were wearing out.

"We were there 'till about 11:30," says Sharshel, the paramedic who had been separated from his friend Bill Barnes since trying to get helicopter service working.

When Sharshel and Barnes finally connected, they just looked blankly at each other.

"I've got to get out of here," Sharshel said.

Barnes replied, "I'm right on your heels."

*"I was just devastated. I couldn't believe it. I didn't have on any shoes, couldn't find any shoes. A big roll of tin was in the middle of the family room."*

–Gereda Edwards

59

Left: The tornado passes near Arkansas City. Photo by Joel Day.

After the tornado, Sam and Hellen Tolleses' home was in fragments. Photo by Keith Tolles.

Sam and Hellen Tolles stand in front of the site of the home where they lived for 54 years. This photo was taken about a week after the tornado. Photo by Arkansas City Daily Traveler.

For those who had been there from the start — seeing so much pain, such severe injuries, so many deaths — the work was beginning to "get to them," Sharshel says.

The pain, in many ways, though, was just beginning. Δ

# Cowley County

For Cowley County, the drama began at 6:30 p.m. A spotter for the National Weather Service reported a tornado six miles west of Arkansas City, and city officials set off the sirens.

At a farm near Arkansas City, Sam and Helen Tolles, both 80, knew about the severe weather alerts, but they didn't worry until Helen looked out the window. Two miles away, what looked like a boiling whitish-gray wall was grinding through their wheatfield. Several vortices fingered the ground like tentacles. The winds within the funnel were swirling at speeds up to 206 miles per hour, according to the Weather Service.

At the same moment, the couple's 39-year-old son, Keith, was in Arkansas City looking toward his parents' farm only four miles away. He saw the the tornado track through the farm fields. Later Keith said he knew that it had to be hitting his parents' farm. Keith hurried to his car and sped toward their home.

At the farm, Helen saw the tornado smash through an electrical substation. Fireballs shot through the whirling mass.

"Sam, come here," Helen yelled. Sam went to the window of their three-bedroom frame house and looked out. He turned and put on his rubber boots. Sam had always told his family that if a tornado ever swept through the farm he and Helen had worked since 1937, he would seek refuge in the old well house near the front door.

Helen ran into the living room to huddle next to the old stove that heated their house. Later, she couldn't explain why they ran in two different directions. There was simply no time to think, Helen says.

Sam had stepped off the porch, one foot on the porch and the other on the ground, and he put his hand on the well-house covering to open it, but the tornado had arrived. He looked up through the center of the funnel, peering into darkness and something that looked like stars.

Boards splintered around Helen. The house was yanked off its foundation, shoved 30 feet and rotated about 30 degrees. The walls and roof exploded. Winds slammed Helen into the wall and threw her under the ironing board. She lost consciousness.

A board smacked Sam in the side of the head, and a piece of a concrete block crashed into his ear and blew away. The tornado thundered across a field away from their house.

The tornado moved northeast, passing over the Pleasant Valley Cemetery and knocking down more than 100 tombstones. It skirted to the south of an airport and industrial park called Strother Field, crossed U.S.

Highway 77 and increased in intensity. The tornado's winds were now whirling as fast as 260 miles per hour, and the path was nearly one-half mile wide.

Stephanie Streeter, a health care worker at a local hospital, and her son Robert, 7, were watching the weather from their home east of Strother Field near the town of Hackney. They were alone because Stephanie's husband, Hardy, had been gone to Winfield earlier in the day to prepare for maneuvers with his National Guard unit.

She and her son were listening to weather bulletins on the radio. At that moment, Stephanie could see only lightning, rain and hail. She dashed to the car and drove it into the garage to protect it from the hail. Shortly after she came back into the house, an announcer on the radio shouted: "Strother Field take cover."

She grabbed pillows, blankets and one of their dogs, a dachshund. She and her son climbed into the bath tub and covered themselves up.

The telephone rang. Stephanie hopped out, ran to the phone and picked it up. It was Hardy calling to warn her about the storm.

"There's a tornado coming," she yelled, hung up and ran back to the tub. She climbed in and wrapped her arms tightly around Robert and the dog. Within seconds the tornado hit.

"You could hear it, feel it," Stephanie says. "It smelled like wet landfill. It stunk horribly."

Water sloshed out of the toilet, and the house vibrated. The roof peeled away and flew clear. Debris fell into the tub. The tornado sucked the tub with all three occupants out of the house, spinning the tub around.

The tub hit ground, hard, knocking the wind out of Stephanie, then the tub still carrying its passengers rose into the air again. Robert clung to his mother so tightly he pulled out a handful of her hair and bruised her shoulder. The tub fell again and bounced twice along the ground, tossing them out. Suction from the wind began pulling Robert straight toward a fence as Stephanie fought to hold onto him, then she blacked out.

The tornado rumbled toward Donna and Marten Morgan's house, two miles east of Winfield. Sitting in their 75-year-old, two-story house, the young couple was watching television coverage of the weather alerts. Donna worked at Winfield State Hospital. Marten was the manager of a farming co-op. They had planned to go bowling that night but changed their plans after the hail came down. Donna says she has a long-standing respect for rough weather. "When it hails, Donna goes to the basement," she says. True to her custom, Donna trotted to the basement and put on a headphone radio. Only then did she hear the reports of a large tornado two miles east of Winfield. She relayed the report to her husband.

"That's us," Marten called back.

"I know," she screamed to him. "Now get down here!"

The two hurried to the southwest corner of the basement and stood near the washer and dryer. They heard the wind battering the house, and Donna began to count, hoping that the storm would pass quickly. By the time she got to 5, the funnel had arrived. She peered out a window and saw a utility pool shaking violently. The couple ran to the opposite corner of the basement,

"You could hear it, feel it. It smelled like wet landfill. It stunk horribly.

–Stephanie Streeter

Debris is piled on and around two cars at the site of what used to be Hardy and Stephanie Streeters' garage. Photo by Barbara Streeter.

Right: The remains of trees and fragments of buildings fill the yard of a damaged house near Arkansas City. Photo by John Decker

*"I didn't see how anybody could have lived through that."*

–Keith Tolles

frantically trying to cover themselves with an old carpet. Donna grabbed Marten around the waist.

"I heard a series of loud booms," she says. The ceiling rose and settled, rose and settled and then flew off, leaving the couple looking into the sky. The two peered up into the funnel. It was gray. Donna could see white arcs that looked as if somebody had painted them with white paint and a paintbrush. Suction from the funnel suddenly pulled at them. It swept items from the basement across the floor and sucked them out of the house. It began pulling Donna toward the other side of the basement. Marten lay across her to hold her down.

The tornado moved on, this time boiling across the fields toward Marilyn Decker's mobile home two miles away from the Morgans' house. Decker, 29, worked as a nurse's aide at Winfield State Hospital and lived alone. Decker missed a ride to a house with a basement, according to a newpaper report. She was trying to take cover in a nearby ditch when the tornado appeared, the report said.

The tornado traveled through the center of Decker's home and ground past Burden. At some point outside of Cowley County, the tornado either lifted off the ground or dissipated. Meteorologists said they weren't certain. The tornado had traveled 25 miles through Cowley County.

Sam Tolles stumbled twice through the debris that had once been his house before he found Helen. Stephanie Streeter awoke to the screaming of her son. Donna and Marten Morgan climbed out of their basement and found their house, all their animals, even

their trees destroyed. The Tolleses, Streeters and Morgans survived with only minor injuries. A neighbor found Marilyn Decker's lifeless body in a pasture near her home. Nothing was left of her mobile home.

After the tornado passed, blood and mud caked Sam Tolles' face. He looked at the house. Nothing was standing except for the walls in one corner. Sam tripped through the debris, but he couldn't find Helen. He turned and walked back through. There she was, lying amid splintered boards and plaster in the one surviving corner of the house.

Helen opened her eyes and saw a ceiling fan lying amid the debris. The fan was still attached to a small strip of ceiling. Around the house, trees lay uprooted or snapped in two.

A group of college-aged men who had been chasing the storm arrived at the Tolleses' place. They were leading Helen to a chair when Keith drove up. The moment before he saw his mother, Keith was frightened. The house looked as if it had been bombed.

"I didn't see how anybody could have lived through that," Keith says.

Except for cuts and bruises, Sam and Helen had survived. "I think God protected us," Helen says.

After the tornado moved away, the first thing Stephanie Streeter heard  was her son's scream. She opened her eyes and found him nearby covered with bits of plaster and thin slats of lath. The tornado had tossed the two over a 4-foot fence into the backyard next door. The bathtub was nowhere in sight.

Stephanie comforted Robert and heard a hissing sound coming from the propane tank near them. She

The debris-filled living room of Lee Kelly's home south of Winfield can be seen at center right. Photo by Jane Laughlen.

tried to shut off the tank, but couldn't. Grabbing Robert, she hustled away. They discovered the body of the dachshund and the body of another one of their dogs, a greyhound.

The roof of their house and bits of the walls were strewn over the fields. Most of the contents of the house had been sucked out.

Eventually, a Highway Patrol trooper found Stephanie and Robert and called an ambulance. They were treated at the hospital where Stephanie worked. At first her coworkers did not recognize her because her face was matted with mud and blood. Once they had cleaned her up, they realized that most of the blood was not from Stephanie. The Streeters never learned where the blood had come from. Stephanie suffered huge bruises on her back and her head was covered with lumps. Scratches and bruises covered Robert.

Hardy wasn't reunited with Stephanie and Robert until he talked his commanding officer into letting him leave his National Guard unit to check on his family. When he arrived at the debris that had been his house, the only person Hardy could find was a reporter. The reporter directed Hardy to the hospital.

The Streeters never found the bathtub that had protected Stephanie and Robert.

The Morgans climbed out of their basement and discovered that practically everything they had owned had been destroyed. The house was gone. Five pigs, two dogs and 48 chickens had perished.

"I stood up and freaked out," Donna says. She looked at the wreckage and cried out, "Not everything. Not everything!" Δ

*"I stood up and freaked out."*

–Donna Morgan

# Elk County

At 7:20 p.m. Elk County Sheriff Janet Lee was watching the sky. A gray wall cloud had formed across the horizon to the southwest. The cloud was boiling with gray wisps, building to a quick swirl and then dissipating.

Lee already had positioned spotters around the county, giving special attention to the border with Cowley County. Few things had scared the 37-year-old sheriff during her term in office, but she was frightened tonight. She had heard reports of the tornado that ravaged Cowley.

"We were out west of Grenola, and one of our spotters spotted a tornado about eight miles west," Lee said. "That would put it in Cowley County. I tried to follow it and I got up on a hill west of (Howard), but I lost sight (of the tornado)."

Within minutes a call came over her radio from a game warden driving along Highway 99. He had seen a tornado drop from the sky seven miles west and two miles east of Howard, the Elk County seat.

The property of L.E. and H.L. Arbuckle was under the tornado, but the brothers were lucky. The funnel did little more than blow trees onto a pickup truck and damage a roof. The brothers were not even home. At this point, the tornado's winds were whirling at speeds estimated to range from 158 to 206 miles per hour.

Right: Before and after photos show the destruction of Olga Jenkins' home north of Howard. The scene before the tornado is shown in the photo at the left. The jagged remains of tornado-ravaged trees and pile of debris mark the site afterwards. Photo by Hazel Moore.

*"Grandpa, do you hear that roar? What is it?"*

–Christy Wells

The funnel moved northeast, damaging roofs and outbuildings as it bounced along, moving "like a pogo stick," Sheriff Lee says.

By the time the funnel reached Aline McKenzie's house, its wind speeds had intensified to as fast as 260 miles per hour. The funnel was a half-mile wide.

"I was watching television alone," McKenzie says. Her husband Bill was at work in Wichita. She had already been alerted to danger by the warnings broadcast on TV. "I was watching to see how close it was to us. After I tracked it across Cowley County, I started to get ready."

Rain and hail the size of golf balls pelted her two-bedroom house and then stopped.

"I looked out, and it looked clear," she says. "Then it started boiling and roiling."

The tornado was hidden behind the hills to the southwest of her house. Almost immediately after the clouds started boiling, she heard an odd humming. McKenzie dashed for the storm cellar under her porch, carrying her purse, a radio, flashlight and a Bible. She crouched in the cellar and prayed. Thirty seconds later her house came apart. A deafening roar surrounded her. The cellar roof flew off. A paint can, stored on shelves below the roof, flew out and exploded. Wooden shelves fell over McKenzie, shielding her from the debris that was raining down around her. Debris fell onto the top steps of the stairway leading to her haven. The steps tilted and cracked, crashing down. Something fell on her radio and smashed it.

Across the road, Jim Wunderlich's 14-year-old granddaughter Christy Wells had been the first to identify the danger.

"Grandpa, do you hear that roar?" she asked him. "What is it?"

"It's just that old wind and hail," he replied, but Wunderlich says that he felt far from certain that he was right. When the sound became louder, the two decided to take shelter, running to a storm cellar as the noise engulfed them.

The tornado skipped through the hills. Less than a mile away, 89-year-old Olga Jenkins looked out the window of her neat, two-story home on a farm that had been owned by her family since 1875. Jenkins watched intently. She was all too familiar with tornados. When she was 13, a tornado had ravaged the farm while she and her family hid in the storm cellar.

Jenkins listened to the radio as she watched. The skies seemed to be clearing. Jenkins was looking south. The tornado was coming from the west. Jenkins did not realize the funnel was on her until she heard glass breaking in the house. It was too late to run to the cellar. She pulled open a closet door and jumped in. Plaster fell around her.

"I never did get excited," Jenkins says. "I probably should have." At some point in the fury, she blacked out.

The tornado barreled northeast, tossing up trees and fences.

Richard Jacobs, 77, and his wife, Lucille, 79 had just arrived home from a social function at their church. Lucille was a quiet woman who was known for her excellent crochet work. Rain and hail had pelted their car during the ride home. Upon reaching their double-wide mobile home, which was set over a basement, the couple listened to the radio and stared out the window.

**Left: Aline McKenzie survived by hiding in this fruit cellar. Photo by John Parker.**

**The tornado ripped the roof off one of the barns on the McKenzie farm. Photo by Buzz Shaddy.**

The hail stopped about the time the signal from the Coffeyville radio station deteriorated into static. Richard asked Lucille to go with him to the basement. She refused. Since the weather appeared to be clearing, the couple walked back to the living room and sat down.

Richard says that he believes he dozed for a few minutes in a chair. He doesn't know whether he was startled awake by the storm or Lucille's scream. When he opened his eyes, the tornado was bursting through the row of trees across the road in front of their house. Richard jumped and ran for the sliding glass doors in the back of their house. Looking over his shoulder, he saw the tornado reach his front door. The house exploded.

The tornado continued across the fields through the sparsely populated edge of the county. It crossed into Greenwood County, weakening into a thin rope-like shape that damaged fences and power lines. Just before reaching Severy, the tornado lifted up, passing over the town as a harmless funnel cloud. It dissipated over the Toronto Reservoir.

When it became quiet, Aline McKenzie discovered that her house had been destroyed, but she was not injured. Jim Wunderlich and his granddaughter were safe, but the door of their storm cellar wouldn't open. Olga Jenkins awoke to jolting pain and injuries that would keep her hospitalized for nine weeks. Dazed, Richard Jacobs walked around the shattered landscape that had been his home. A sheriff's deputy found the body of Lucille in a field more than 70 feet from where she had been sitting. Richard Jacobs was hospitalized for 10 days.

At the wreckage of the McKenzie house, Aline crawled out of the cellar and found that her home had been heaved 30 yards from its foundation. A complete set of kitchen cabinets — still attached to the wall — jutted out of an otherwise demolished heap. The roof — chimney still intact — rested on the ground. The jagged remnants of 17 trees were scattered across the yard. Her freezer was hurled hundreds of yards across a road. The Bible had been tossed into a nearby pasture.

Across the street at the Wunderlich house, grandfather and granddaughter did not believe much had happened until they tried to open the cellar door. It hardly moved.

"I just kept a shoving and a pushing," Wunderlich says. He used his long, lean body and strong arms to free the door. The pair climbed out and looked around. Debris had been piled onto the roof of the cellar; debris filled the yard, but the Wunderlich house still stood.

When Jenkins first awoke, she could not move. Fishing line had wrapped her in a cocoon. She lay 30 feet from the closet where she had sought refuge. Debris covered her body. Plaster filled her mouth.

"I leaned up on my elbow and I thought, 'Oh me.'"

The left side of her torso was crushed. Four ribs and a punctured lung ached. Her collar bone and shoulder blades had been broken.

The house and barn were devastated. Tall trees had been snapped. Whole sections of hedge row had been leveled. Neighbors found Jenkins and rushed her to the hospital.

When Richard Jacobs came to, he was standing up. He moved like a man in a daze. The first thing he

*"I leaned up on my elbow and I thought, 'Oh me!"*

–Olga Jenkins

At 9 on the morning after the tornado, the Welborn home near Meriden was surrounded by wreckage. About 1/3 of the home was sliced away by the tornado. Photo by Gloria Harrington.

*"He looked like he came out of a coal mine. His face was black and his eyes were rimmed in red."*

–Sheriff Janet Lee

remembers is walking around what had once been his house.

"I walked around the house and shut the propane off," Richard says.

When rescuers arrived soon afterward, Richard was walking down the road.

"He looked like he came out of a coal mine," Sheriff Lee says. "His face was black and his eyes were rimmed in red."

He had cuts across his face and shoulder. A 6-inch U-shaped gash on his ankle was cut to the bone.

The contents of the Jacobs house was strewn for miles. His van had been overturned and twisted. His combine had been thrown into what had once been his basement and was now an open pit. Rescuers remember seeing Lucille's colorful yarn hanging from the broken branches of the trees not far from where rescuers found her body.

As the sun set and rain fell, residents struggled with the aftermath. Fallen trees clogged roads. Ambulances had to weave in and out of shallow ditches to reach the injured. Atmospheric interference cut off Sheriff Lee's radio communication with her office in Howard for about 45 minutes. It was unlike anything she had ever faced before.

"After the tornado, with everything being so dark and trees everywhere in the road, it was like being in another world," Lee says. Δ

## Jefferson & Atchison Counties

The horror of April 26 would not end for hours. Far north of the chaos in south-central Kansas, a tornado formed just outside the Weather Service office at Billard Airport in Topeka. The wind outside the door was nearly calm, while a wind-speed indicator 250 yards away read 56 knots, about 64 miles per hour. The funnel damaged a power substation near U.S. Highway 24 and then tracked into Jefferson County. It was 9 p.m.

A little more than 4 miles from the small Jefferson County town of Meriden, Danny Welborn, the manager of Meriden's farm Co-op, his wife Brenda and their two sons, Lance, 19, and Layne, 14, heard a broadcast report that a tornado had been spotted at Billard Airport. The tornado was moving northeast.

The Welborns knew it was only a matter of minutes before the tornado arrived at their home. Lance grabbed a 2-month-old basset hound to protect it. The whole family ran out of their mobile home in search of shelter. They only made it to the porch. The tornado had arrived at their driveway. "We ran right into it," Brenda says.

Danny says, "The tornado sucked the porch up from under us."

Danny blacked out. Brenda, Layne and Lance, still holding onto the dog, tumbled off the porch.

A car with its wheel in the air rests in the front yard of Louise Noll's house in Nortonville. Photo by Greg Wagner.

Left: The living room of the Mauzey house is a gutted shell after the tornado. Only rafters and rectangles of insulation mark where the roof had been. The living room floor and all the furniture fell into the basement. Photo by Doris Mountain.

The funnel ground away from their house. It finally rose into the clouds four miles west of the town of Ozawkie.

At 9:30 p.m. a second tornado touched down in the countryside 5 miles southwest of Nortonville and churned toward town.

About two miles down the path, Joe Bonnel, a farmer, was alone in the farmhouse he shared with his mother Deloris. His mother was at work at the Hallmark plant in Leavenworth. Joe was on the patio on the east side of the house when he saw the funnel coming. The tornado burst out through a hedge row and Joe took off running for the basement. He was running as fast as he could, but he felt as if he were being pulled backward. Joe pounded down the steps. He was at the second step from the bottom when the tornado hit. A pipe flew through the air and hit him in the side.

The tornado careened to the northeast. Nortonville Fire Chief Kenny Weishaar and his group of weather spotters had taken a break after hours of searching the sky for storms.

"I decided nothing was going to happen," Weishaar says.

But then his radio carried the voice of a firefighter in nearby Valley Falls. The man had sighted a tornado and it was heading straight for Nortonville. Weishaar radioed his wife, Mary Ann, to sound Nortonville's siren.

Judy Keirns, a teacher in the Winchester school district, had always been leery of storms. That afternoon she had been closely watching the sky. She was home with her three children, aged 5 to 14, when the siren sounded. Her husband Joe was at a plumbing convention in Topeka. Judy and her children ran to the basement of their home in Nortonville. The lights went off. Judy grabbed a mattress and barricaded everyone under the stairwell. "We said the Lord's Prayer," she says.

They were engulfed in the roar of the wind. They heard a loud boom, boom.

When the weather became threatening Rachel Rauth grabbed a 90-year-old quilt and $900 and went to her sister-in-law Louise Noll's house nearby. A few minutes later Rauth left Noll's house and headed for Harriet Whitaker's house to pick up the 88-year-old woman and take her to safety at Noll's home. Leona Kooser, a neighbor, arrived at Noll's house after hearing storm warnings on television. When the siren sounded, all four went to the basement. They heard a crash and bang. Rauth made the sign of the cross.

"We all prayed," Kooser says.

The tornado swirled out of Nortonville and headed for the Jefferson-Atchison county line.

At Steve and Lanell Mauzey's house on the Atchison side of the county line, warning came from the television. The family was eating a late dinner so they grabbed their food and headed for the basement. They felt safe downstairs. Steve, a pharmacist in Atchison, Lanell, their daughters Ginger, 12, and Arlene, 15, relaxed. Arlene sat down on the end of the couch to do her homework.

A low rumble filled their house. It sounded as if a huge truck was rolling over them, Steve says. All four members of the family raced into a closet under the stairs. Above them came cracking and snapping and a

*"We all prayed."*

–Leona Kooser

Pews still sit in straight rows the morning after the tornado tore the roof and most of the walls off the Baptist Church in Nortonville. Photo by Ken Weishaar.

swishing sound.

The tornado rumbled to the northeast. It thundered through several farms before finally dissipating near Doniphan County. The tornado had been on the ground for 25 miles.

> *"I couldn't believe it."*
>
> –Judy Keirns

After the roar of the tornado, Brenda, Lance and Layne Welborn scrambled through the debris that filled their yard to find Danny. He had been flung 60 feet from the trailer and landed next to his pickup truck. Danny remembers little else except that he was drifting in and out of consciousness as they reached him. Brenda's wrist hurt, and Lane was bleeding from gashes in his leg and head. Around them were the bits and pieces of their home. Half of it had been blown away.

A neighbor brought his truck around and loaded Danny and Lance next to him in the cab. Brenda and Layne sat in the open in the back as the pickup bounced through the 35-minute drive to Stormont-Vail Medical Center in Topeka.

At the hospital, the family learned that Danny had suffered a broken hip and cracked vertebra in his back. Brenda had a broken wrist. Lance required 12 stitches to close his gashes. Neither Layne nor the dog he was carrying were injured.

The Welborns' mobile home had been picked up and spun around. A pet rabbit who had been inside an unlatched cage in the living room was discovered free on a kitchen counter top. Inside the cage, there was a kitchen canister.

At the Bonnel farm outside of Nortonville, the 89-year-old house, five barns and a garage had been destroyed.

Joe suffered a bruised spleen. The eardrums of his 11-year-old German shorthair pointer had burst.

At the Keirns' house, the family emerged when they heard the sqwak of a walkie-talkie and the voice of a friend warning them that there might be a gas leak.

"I couldn't believe it," Judy Keirns says. One side of their car was caved in. The garage door was on it. The house had been lifted off its foundation. Part of the roof was gone. Three huge trees that had been in the front yard had been destroyed. Limbs had crashed through a picture window and part of a living room wall.

Friends invited the family to take shelter in the local funeral home to stay until Keirns husband, Joe, returned home. Before leaving the wreckage of the house, Judy left a note. The note said, "Joe, we've gone to the funeral home."

When Joe arrived home, he saw the damage and ran upstairs and downstairs without finding his family. He saw the note and panicked. When he arrived at the funeral home, Joe hugged his family and cried.

At the house where Rauth, Noll, Whitaker and Kooser had taken cover, neighbors, helped the women climb out of the basement. When they reached the surface, they realized the house had split in two, the floor cracking and falling downward to form a giant "V". The point of the "V" rested in the basement near the place where the four women had been hiding.

Whitaker suffered a cut in her arm that required five stitches. She says she has no idea how she got it. The other women were not harmed.

In the Mauzeys' house, Steve Mauzey was the first person to climb upstairs to survey the damage. He came

**A coloring book about Kansas is covered with broken glass on the floor in the Mauzey house. Photo by Steve Mauzey.**

back into the basement to tell his family, "Don't be shocked at what you see when you get up here."

Lanell followed her husband up the steps; the girls were close behind.

"I didn't know what to think for a minute," Lanell says.

The roof had vanished. Part of the fireplace had fallen, causing the floor to give way in the living room. The garage and a shed were missing.

Several minutes later the family discovered that a couch and coffee table from the first floor had crashed through the broken flooring and smashed down on the couch in the basement. The place that had been crushed was the spot where Arlene had been sitting only seconds before the tornado hit.

By now Fire Chief Kenny Weishaar had reached the fire station. He started a generator, got a base radio station and a telephone working. "Then I started giving orders," Weishaar says.

It was now almost 20 hours since meteorologists had first worried about the troubling forecast for the day. No more tornadoes were sighted. The terror of April 26 was finally over. Δ

*"I started giving orders."*

–Fire Chief Kenny Weishaar

# The Drama Continues

*"She just kept dropping kids into the pit until it was full," Lolita says. "And then she asked, "Is there any room for me? If not, I love my children...just save my children."*

On May 16, just as a tornado was closing in on the Roy and Lolita Carder farmstead in Hodgeman County, Sandy Ontiveros drove into the yard looking for safety for herself and her children. Lolita heard the honk of the car, poked her head out of the well pit where she had taken cover, and motioned for Ontiveros and her children to join her. Ontiveros drove over and started putting the children into the pit.

–story page 74

One of the many tornadoes that rumbled through Kansas on April 26, roars through Washington County near the town of Washington. Photo by Dallas Beikmann.

# Other Storms of 1991

The injuries and destruction of the 1991 storm season extended throughout Kansas. On April 26, for example, dozens of tornadoes touched down besides the tornadoes that ravaged Sedgwick and Butler, Elk, Cowley, Jefferson and Atchison counties. On that day, damaging twisters also struck Washington, Wabaunsee and Woodson counties. Goddard in Sedgwick County was hit.

But storms disrupted lives throughout the spring. On April 11, a tornado in Stockton injured one woman. On May 4, hail shredded gardens in Everest in Brown County. On May 16, a tornado terrified residents of Sedgwick County as it paralleled the path of the April 26 tornado. Other twisters on May 16 tore through homes in rural Hodgeman County. May 27 windstorms injured campers at Wilson State Park while farther west an unexpected blizzard forced officials to close Interstate 70, the main east-west highway in the state. On June 15, lightning sparked a fire that destroyed a landmark building at the University of Kansas.

*"It was just like I was floating."*

–Duane Pfannenstiel

## April 11

Ernestine Swaney was seriously injured and three rural homes were destroyed by a tornado that cut a half-mile-wide path of destruction through Stockton, according to *the Salina Journal.*

Swaney was in the basement of her home when she was struck by a heavy timber. A few feet away was an El Camino truck that was flung through the air by the tornado. The homes of Don Schneider and Roy and Louisa Morain were also reduced to rubble.

The newspaper reported that Kansas Highway Patrol Trooper Duane Pfannenstiel's patrol car was lifted by the storm. The trooper says he was driving south of Stockton when his engine suddenly stopped and he lost control of the steering. Later, a trucker who watched the incident would report that the car rose into the air.

"I didn't know I was off the ground until I talked to him," Pfannenstiel told the newspaper. "It was a weird experience. It was just like I was floating, like I had no control at all of the vehicle." Δ

People inspect the ruins of the Schuessler home on the day after the tornado. Photo by Kevin Graves.

Right: The tornado damaged trees around Dorothy Rollman's house near the town of Washington. Photo by Undersheriff Michael Hood.

Mildred Schuessler (left), daughter-in-law Kim (right) and their children took cover in Mildred's basement. Photo by Stan Thiessen.

**April 26**

# The Other Tornadoes

Washington County first heard about the danger at 3:10 p.m. when Sheriff J. Wiley Kerr got a call from the National Weather Service office in Concordia. Radar had detected a problem in a storm cell near Clifton. Within minutes, weather spotters near Palmer reported that a funnel was on the ground and heading toward Washington.

At the Schuessler place in rural Washington County, Stephanie Schuessler, 6, had just arrived home from school. Shortly after she walked into her parents' double-wide mobile home, hail fell. Stephanie was the first to insist that her mother, Kim, and the three other Schuessler children go next door to seek safer shelter at the house of her grandmother, Mildred Schuessler, 77. Stephanie carefully wrapped her kitten in a blanket and walked across the yard to the house. As they arrived, Kim looked to the southwest and saw the tornado. Mildred went to the front door to see for herself.

"As I watched, more tornadoes dropped," Mildred says. "There were three of them swinging back and forth."

The family hastened to the basement. Kim barely made it because she had stopped to answer the telephone. The call had come from her husband, Mike, who was warning her of the tornado.

As the family cowered behind a concrete wall that was built to be their storm shelter, they heard a blast. The lights went out.

Bending over the children to protect them, Mildred saw the darkness give way to light again. She told Kim the power must have come back on. Kim said, "That's not lights, that's the sky."

When the family emerged from its hiding place, they discovered that two of their cars had been crumpled and flung hundreds of yards into a field. Heavy farm machinery was mangled and strewn over the ground.

Across the street from the Schuesslers, the tornado shattered windows at the home of Ken and Mary Jane Schoen and then smashed a small cemetery just south of U.S. 36. The twister narrowly missed a business, Bekemeyer Enterprises, which raises livestock. It churned through the Rollman property. Dorothy survived by taking shelter in the basement. When she emerged, she first wondered why her car was not in the garage. Then she realized that the garage had been blown 50 feet from its foundation. Rollman's car was undamaged.

The tornado stayed on the ground for six more miles as it passed to the west of Washington, then it lifted back into the sky for 12 miles before setting down again northwest of Hanover.

Verla Kruse stood at the entrance to their basement and watched as her husband Harold, 71, and her son struggled against the suction of the tornado to get to safety. Harold had been photographing the funnel and when he tried to get to the basement he found that he needed his son's help to move against the wind.

The front of a tractor can be seen in a damaged barn on Harold Kruse's farm near Hanover. Photo by Ken Stohe.

Right: John and Barb Juenemans' children examine the damage to the Lanham grain elevator, which they own. The tornado struck the town that straddles the Nebraska-Kansas line. Photo by Barb Jueneman.

"If my son hadn't been there, my husband probably wouldn't have made it to the shelter," Verla says.

All three family members made it to the basement. When the tornado passed, dust filtered lazily downward dimming the lights as the family started up the stairs.

"Halfway up the steps we stopped," Verla says. "My son turned and said, 'Everything is gone.' "

When Verla emerged she saw that their house remained, but 18 buildings that had been on their property had been destroyed.

Among the other Washington County farms hardest hit were those owned by Robert Rohlfs, Fred Grefe and James Wiese near Lanham.

Rhohlfs says he did not see a funnel but took cover after something smashed a window in his house. The wind blew apart two garages, two machine sheds, a barn and a brooder house and caused major damage to his home, chicken shed and machinery.

Fred Grefe's son Delbert saw the storm approach and the family took shelter in a basement. Although Fred Grefe's house had only minor damage, Delbert's nearby farm sustained major damage. Across the road from the Fred Grefe farm, James Wiese lost a barn, garage, granary and machine shed. His home was extensively damaged. Before sweeping out of Kansas, the tornado roared through the town of Lanham, damaging the office at the Lanham elevator and crumpling grain bins. Lanham residents also reported damage to three homes.

On April 26, other tornadoes damaged houses in Goddard and destroyed Hi-Tech Performance, a boat business owned by Duane Oblander, according to newspaper accounts. Julie and Dale Maben and their four children narrowly escaped injury when the storm blew apart their house.

In Wabaunsee County, a farm house and some buildings near Lake Wabaunsee were destroyed by a tornado that tracked through the county and then moved into Shawnee County, according to the Weather Service. The tornado cut through the western edge of Rossville, damaging several homes before moving into Jackson County where it dissipated. Near the town of Maple Hill, the tornado damaged a stone shurch that was built in 1876.

In Woodson County another tornado caused an estimated $300,000 in damage when it struck a rock quarry and a farmhouse north of Toronto, the Weather Service reported. At the quarry, equipment and trucks received the major damage. A tanker truck, full of fuel and weighing up to 40,000 pounds, was reportedly blown 75 yards by the tornado. The funnel picked up a farmhouse and turned it 90 degrees before setting it down, the Weather Service reported.    Δ

The tornado that thundered through Washington County takes on a whispy look as it passes near Beatrice, Nebraska. Photo by Shayde Goracke.

Oral Glunt stands next to his Chevrolet pickup at his home in Hodgeman County. Photo by Stan Thiessen

Lolita Carder (left) points to the entrance to the well pit where she, a neighbor and the neighbor's four chidlren survived the tornado. Photo by Stan Thiessen

The tornado twisted this nail around a woven strand of wire on the Carder farm. Photo by Stan Thiessen.

# May 4

More than an inch of hail pummeled the small Brown County town of Everest and surrounding area in the early afternoon, heavily damaging wheat crops, gardens and scouring the paint off houses.

Cool temperatures allowed the hail to remain on the ground throughout the afternoon. By evening, some drifts of hailstones still had not melted.

"Have you ever seen anything like this?" asked the *Everest World.* Δ

# May 16

The 16th was a frightening day, particularly in Sedgwick, Butler and Hodgeman counties.

For Sedwick and Bulter counties, it seemed like a recurring nightmare as tornadoes again struck the area, including one funnel that nearly retraced the path of the fatal storm of April 26. But on May 16 there were no serious injuries. Damge was estimated at $1 million as the tornado danced through the southern sections of the Wichita metropolitan area, the Weather Service reported. At least 20 homes were damaged.

In Hodgeman County, Oral Glunt, 72, felt the first sign of danger through a metal wire attached to the windmill on his farm 13 miles west of Jetmore. At the time, Glunt was attempting to fix the windmill by fiddling with its shut-off mechanism. He glanced at the rumbling storm front as it approached from the west but went back to work because it did not look threatening. As he worked at the mechanism, he felt a jolt in his neck. A mild electrical current apparently sparked by nearby lightning had jumped from a wire attached to the mechanism to his neck. Glunt was not injured, but he says he thought that the shock was a good sign that

dangerous lightning was on its way. Glunt climbed into his pickup truck, and headed for home.

As Glunt pulled into his farmyard, he still could not see the tornado. But as he entered his house, the windows around him shattered, then the tornado was gone. The house was slightly damaged. A shed was destroyed and some telephone polls and trees were snapped. Glunt was not injured.

At the Carder place, Roy Carder was two miles from his home working on his farm. His wife, Lolita, was in the kitchen, baking cinnamon rolls. From the kitchen window, she could see a storm coming and wondered if her husband had noticed it.

"I went out to see where he was," Lolita says. By then, the tornado was closing on the house. Lolita says she scrambled into a well pit in their yard. The pit was lined with concrete and contained the water pump for their well.

From the pit, Lolita suddenly heard the honk of a car horn. It was her neighbor Sandy Ontiveros trying to find safety for herself and her four children. Poking her head out of the opening, Lolita motioned for Ontiveros to bring the children.

The tornado took the walls of Larry McKibben's barn in Hodgeman County. McKibben was 1/4 mile away from the farm in a tractor when the tornado hit. Photo by Dodge City Weather Service.

**Right:** Shot from what was once the interior of Larry Mckibben's barn, this photo shows his house, which received little damage on the tornado. Photo by Dodge City Weather Service.

"She just kept dropping kids into the pit until it was full," Lolita says. "And, then she asked, 'Is there any room for me? If not, I love my children ... just save my children.' But we made room for her."

Heading home in his pickup truck, Roy attempted to beat the storm, but the storm appeared to block his path. Roy circled the driveway, heading for the safety of the machine shed, but when he stopped next to the garage and tried to open the truck door, the wind forced Roy back inside the cab. Moments later, the garage blew apart.

Neither Roy nor any of the people on his farm were injured. "The good Lord was with us," Roy says.

At the McKibbin farm, Larry McKibben was in the enclosed cab of his tractor when the storm overtook him. A black cloud covered the ground. There was no funnel in sight, McKibbin says.

He jumped from his tractor to hide in a pump house, but as he started toward it, the small building flew over his head and disappeared into the blackness. The sprinkler system attached to the pump house was destroyed.

McKibbin survived. The Weather Service reported later that he was far luckier than he had first imagined.

"Mr. McKibbin's account indicates the main vortex apparently passed directly over him, while a suction vortex destroyed much of his farmstead," the Weather Service reports. "Mr. McKibben certainly ranks as one of the luckier individuals alive today as the suction vortex apparently moved just north of him after toppling the sprinkler system." Δ

*"Mr. McKibbin's account indicates the main vortex apparently passed directly over him, while a suction vortex destroyed much of his farmstead."*

–The Weather Service

# May 26

Twelve people received minor injuries when 70 mile-per-hour winds swept through camp grounds at Wilson State Park.

One of the most frightening incidents of the day happened at the camp site of Sylvia and Jim Trogdon of Derby and their friend Kathy Frey and her son Josh, 12, of Wichita. The Trogdons' 7-year-old son Stanley and their 6-month-old daughter Miranda were also along on the trip.

The group was camping on a bluff overlooking Wilson Lake. It was dark and Stanley and Josh had already gone to sleep in a two-man tent. When a light rain began to fall, the adults decided to move into their shelter, a pop-up camper, Sylvia says. The camper has a metal base and a canvas pop-up top. Within 15 minutes, the winds picked up.

"It was like somebody turned on a wind machine," Sylvia says.

A gust of wind rocked the camper.

"I sat up and said to my husband, 'Oh God, should we get out?'"

Immediately, a second gust rocked them, then a third gust blew the camper over, pinning Kathy Frey underneath.

"I remember my husband screaming at me to get out, get out!" Sylvia says. "In the back of our mind was the

Far from the fire, smoke is clearly visible in the sky above the University of Kansas as Hoch Auditorium burns. Photographer G. Mark Smith titled this picture "STOP!!"

Smoke billows out of Hoch Auditorium after a fire was sparked by lightning that struck the University of Kansas landmark. Photo by Rodney Price.

*"We have witnessed the passing of an old and dependable friend."*

–Gene Budig

fact that we weren't far from the bluff."

Taking her baby with her, Sylvia crawled out of the camper into the pouring rain and looked for the tent which had housed the two boys. After a frantic search, she found the tent and made her way to it.

"The wind was blowing so hard that when I was walking to the tent, I was afraid it would blow me off my feet."

The wind had pulled the tent pegs out of the ground and the tent had collapsed. The only thing keeping it from blowing off the bluff into the lake was the boys' weight. To keep the tent from blowing into the water, Sylvia lay down on the tent. She held her baby underneath her in an attempt to shield the baby from the pouring rain. All the while, Sylvia says she shouted at the boys to stay down. The wind was so strong it could have blown them off the bluff if they had stood up, Sylvia says.

While Sylvia was struggling to keep the boys safe, her husband Jim, was attempting to push the camper off Kathy Frey, whose leg was pinned underneath. He was only able to free her when friends, who were camping nearby, came to help.

Despite the trauma of the night, None of the people involved were seriously injured. Kathy Frey suffered severe bruises on her leg, Sylvia says.

Looking back at the incident months later, Sylvia says she still shakes when she talks about it. "I told my husband that I didn't think I'd go camping ever again if there was talk of anything but a rain shower," she says. "We dreamed about it for months afterwards."

On the same day near the western border of the state, a spring snowstorm closed schools, Associated Press reported. Between 2 and 4 inches of snow fell. Winds gusting up to 64 miles per hour reduced visibility to close to zero. Segments of Interstate 70, one of the main east-west routes of the region, were closed between Hays and the Colorado border.

"You know how March is," Salina truck driver Paul LaPorte told the AP. "You never know what it's going to do tomorrow. Yesterday, it was 86 degrees and here this morning it's snowing." Δ

## June 15

The University of Kansas lost a landmark when lightning ignited a fire that destroyed 64-year-old Hoch Auditorium, which served for years as the home of championship Jayhawk basketball teams. In 1955, the building was converted into a 3,500-seat auditorium and classrooms.

Up to 100 firefighters from five cities were called in to fight the fire, which was out of control for nearly three hours. The fire produced a column of black smoke that could be seen 10 miles outside of Lawrence.

"Hoch Auditorium was an important part of the 125-year history of the University of Kansas," Chancellor Gene Budig says. "We have witnessed the passing of an old and dependable friend." Δ

Twisted trees line the road across the street from the Kiser home on Andover. Photo by Janet Kiser.

Right: The Lawrence family in Andover raised the flag and put up a sign to tell the world that they were O.K. Photo by Lynn and Neil Ziegler.

# Aftermath
When the tornadoes passed out of the lives of the survivors, the emergency ended. The long struggle to rebuild began.

For most, the immediate task was to check on the safety of neighbors and friends and to seek medical care for the injured. Soon afterward, people began a frantic search for their possessions.

Sometimes searching in rain and mud, sometimes in the dark, the survivors pawed through mounds of rubble.

In the first hours after the tornado rumbled through Andover, Janet Kiser picked about 20 of her husband's ties out of a tree from which her nightgown and matching robe fluttered on distant branches.

Suzie Storrer found a pair of pants in a tree; she wore them three days straight.

The fiercest searches were for photographs, mementos — as Charlene Fairman says, "anything to prove we had a life before then."

*"Does your daughter need some tender loving care?"*

–Rhonda Neussen

Some were lucky; a neighbor found and returned Suzie Storrer's wedding ring to her within a couple of days. Some never even found their cars.

As the search continued, friends showed up and offered their homes, their eyes, their muscles. Within an hour of the tornado, friends arrived and offered the Rockstads the use of a vacant rental property they owned.

When they heard about the tornado and the damage in Andover, Duane and Rhonda Neussen of Valley Center loaded up a generator, portable lights, food, jackets, drinks, plastic bags and drove to help. The Neussens found the Storrers. The two families had never met before.

"Does your daughter need some tender loving care?" Rhonda Neussen asked Suzie Storrer. When Storrer said yes, Neussen presented her daughter Kelsey with a new, white teddy bear.

Storrer's 72-year-old mother also showed up to help, despite the fact that she lives 90 minutes away and had to get through police barricades. Her mother drove quickly from her home in Emporia and when she found the road blocked, she started walking to find her family. A Highway Patrol trooper who tried to dissuade her ended up delivering Storrer's mother to the Storrer home site.

Andover Mayor Jack Finlason listens to complaints from town residents. Photo by Tom Shoening.

Right: Workers take a break at a Red Cross shelter set up in Faith Baptist Church in Andover. Photo by LuVerne Paine.

*"Everybody in Andover helped."*

−Janet Kiser

For most survivors, the first night after the tornado was difficult. Most people slept at the homes of friends or relatives, some at hotels. Many hardly slept; many barely tried.

"I walked the floor all night," says Kathleen Long. She stayed with a friend the first night. "I got a two-hour nap," says Police Sgt. Paul Troy See. "I was afraid (my son and husband) would be gone if I went to sleep," Charlene Fairman says.

A few stayed at their homes after sending their children to stay with friends. The Kisers stayed in their basement. The Fairmans went to a motel. The Storrers slept in their cars, despite the night's chill.

On the mornings after the tornadoes, the survivors were out early and in force to reclaim bits of their lives. Worn and weary, most wore their only unharmed possessions.

Duane Neussen slipped Suzie Storrer a $20 bill and said, "You have yourselves a good breakfast."

Janet Kiser's brother-in-law brought his truck to haul away whatever could be salvaged. "Everybody in Andover helped," Kiser says.

At the Rockstad home, the kitchen wall with cabinets still attached rested in the back yard. The stemware inside survived, except for one glass. A favorite coat, a fake fur, was in the bathtub.

Merchants in damaged shops tried to clean up and cover windows. Throughout the area, utility companies struggled to restore service. At least 50,000 people in Sedgwick and Butler counties were without power for the weekend after the tornado. Hundreds of utility poles had been destroyed. In some areas, the water supply had been cut and telephone service was out.

Official helpers sent reinforcements. The Red Cross, the Salvation Army, the Federal Emergency Management Agency and 1,500 volunteers from the Mennonite Disaster Service showed up. MDS provided primarily manual labor, helping people sift through the rubble and clear debris. People who had learned about disasters after the Hesston tornado a year before helped volunteers in Andover set up a food bank.

Volunteers brought boxes, plastic bags and tools. They dug, they pushed, carried, hauled and packaged.

By Sunday, only two days after the tornado struck her hometown, Verna Abercrombie of Andover found herself leading the efforts of volunteers for the Andover Recovery Committee.

"You get your immediate needs taken care of, then your secondary needs," Abercrombie says. The immediate needs were as basic as underwear, medicine and, of course, food.

In Wichita and Andover, nine service centers were set up in churches and schools to help homeless storm victims. Feeding stations were created and clothing banks were organized. *The Wichita Eagle* printed telephone numbers that people could call to get help. Other telephone numbers were also printed for people who wanted to offer assistance.

People throughout the state and the nation wanted to help. They just needed a cue, and then they responded quickly. "It was ask, and you will receive," Abercrombie says.

The operators of Ed's Grocery in Andover opened their doors and said, "Take what you need,"

Bill Hamelau (left). Midway Kansas Red Cross Chapter chief operating officer; Elizabeth Dole, president of the American Red Cross; and Pat Hanrahan, president of United Way of the Plains; tour a Red Cross Service Center. Photo by Roger Bain.

Right: Volunteers get food from a Red Cross Emergency Response Vehicle. Photo by Kalen Larson.

Abercrombie says.

Carol Hamill, owner of Carol's Kitchen restaurant, moved her whole operation to the Andover middle school and served thousands of meals. Her restaurant was destroyed by the tornado.

In the Timber Lane area of Haysville, Donna and Tony Tobler at first thought that no one was coming to help.

"We looked up and by noon Saturday, we had about 30 of our friends here and people in my backyard picking up stuff and debris," Donna says. "There were people that I'd never known before ... They were wonderful."

A woman who lived near Timber Lane made ham sandwiches and hot dogs and then circulated through the neighborhood, Linda Lunsford says.

"She'd say, 'How many people do you have? Ten? And she'd hand out 10 sandwiches," Lunsford says.

Other tornado survivors were able to salvage a party–even if it was a brief one. After the tornado, Cheryl Contreras and her neighbor Shereen Wilson discovered that the tornado had deposited 16 barbeque grills in Contreras' backyard in Wichita. Most of the grills were in good shape. Since the meat in the freezer was thawing because the electricity was out, Contreras and Wilson decided to throw a party.

"We barbecued the next day and invited the neighbors over," Contreras says.

At Cox Farm in south Wichita, at least 150 friends and customers showed up to help. People who worked with Ron Stein's wife, Vickie, at Towne West Mall, walked more than a mile every day for a week to bring sandwiches, beverages and other food. Vickies's co-

workers had to walk because the area was sealed off to cars.

"Jenny Clements, the mall manager, took off her shoes — took them right off her feet — and gave them to our daughter," Ron says.

One of Cox' customers, a wheat farmer from Anthony took time from his farm and worked at Cox for two days. The farmer never even told Stein his name.

Despite the help, the search for anything to salvage was frustrating.

"The next day we brought plastic sacks and stuff," Kathleen Long says. She lived at the mobile home park in Andover. "It was just terrible, terribly hard even to find the spot. We saw pieces of wallpaper that identified what was what.

"The landmarks were gone. All you could see was the gravel drives... I salvaged very little compared with what I had. I found two carnival glass heirlooms... I never found any jewelry. I did find some clothes."

Suzie Storrer claims she took things out of a dumpster as fast as her husband put them in. Liz Spencer was lucky enough to find some jewelry.

"It just went to the ground," she says. "I found a Christmas decoration and my necklace was tangled up inside of it."

Before the tornado, the decoration had been in a box in a separate room from the necklace. The discovery was one of the greatest joys of the hard days after the tornado, Spencer says.

Anger was also a part of the aftermath. At Golden Spur, survivors were cleared from the park a few hours after the tornado struck. The next day they were not

*"It was just terrible, terribly hard even to find the spot. We saw pieces of wallpaper that identified what was what."*

–Kathleen Long

Students at Andover Middle School help unload donations to the Donated Household Center set up at the school. Photo by Tom Schoening.

Right: Rick Wagner talks to two teenagers only about 40 minutes after the tornado destroyed his trailer on Golden Spur Mobile Home Park. Wagner was in the trailer when the storm hit and crawled out afterwards. Photo by Tom Schoening.

Robert Meininger's body was found in the Golden Spur Mobile Home Park in the rubble in front of the man pictured. Photo by Gary Bearden.

allowed back into the park until late afternoon. Emergency personnel were combing the area for survivors — or victims.

"We were hoping to get the gore over with," Sgt. See says.

Long says, "That was horrible, standing there and waiting."

See says, "People were getting so angry it looked like we were on the verge of a riot."

At 4 p.m. on the day after the tornado, officials finally let people into Golden Spur.

Some people, like Tony McCrary, became even angrier when they discovered what had happened in the park while they were kept waiting outside.

Immediately after the tornado, Tony had found his car, battered but operable. When he finally got back into Golden Spur, the car was gone. Other residents of the mobile home park also complained about the use of heavy equipment to search for survivors. Possessions that had been salvaged the night before and left in people's yards had been smashed by the treads of the loaders. Officials said later that they had to use the equipment.

"We were lifting things up (with front-end loaders) to find what was underneath," See says. "There were bodies under the wreckage. We had search dogs. When they determined something, we had to lift up and see what was under there... What were we to do? ... It was a no-win situation."

Despite officials efforts to save people from the horror, the residents of Golden Spur discovered a body 15 minutes after the park's gates were opened.

It was Robert Meininger. His wife discovered the body. His daughter, Teresa Warren, fainted at the sight. Warren says the body looked like it had been run over by the heavy machinery officials were using to search the park.

Later some people in Andover would complain that they had not been given adequate warning of the tornado because the city's only siren had failed. When the tornado was approaching Andover, city officials tried unsuccessfully to sound the siren, but nothing happened. To warn residents, officials ordered police officers and firefighters to drive with sirens blaring up and down city streets.

After the tornado, Andover officials would learn that the flow of emergency radio traffic had somehow blocked the dispatcher's radio signal from reaching the siren. Mayor Jack Finlason defended the use of police and fire sirens, saying they were commonly used to warn of tornadoes in the past.

The aftermath of the tornadoes had an even darker side. Andover Detective Alan Sherry says police started hearing reports of looting on Saturday night, the night after the tornado hit Wichita and Andover.

"There were some strange people around my house," Storrer says.

The housing sites on both sides of the Storrers' were looted on Saturday night, she says. The remnants of her house were left untouched as Suzie and her husband slept in a recreational vehicle parked in front.

In Cowley County, a constant stream of cars made it impossible for Jerald and Jimalene Cale to sleep. Some of the cars stopped, the people got out and took things

Bottled water donated by Dillions stands in neat rows at the Red Cross shelter set up in the White Elementary School in Wichita. Photo by Roger Bain.

Right: Rick and Michelle Wagner and their family stand near the only belongings they were able to salvage from their home on Andover Road. Photo by Tom Schoening.

from the rubble of the Cale's house.

"They thought they were picking up souvenirs," Jerald says. "But it was looting in my book."

One suspicious van with Sumner County plates kept driving by and Jerald tried to run it off. Finally he shot at them with a shotgun. The van left.

Some people apparently stole from the dead.

"I hope you say something about the very sad part about people who came and ripped off corpses, people who came afterward," says Pat Kanavy, whose husband and son died. Severely injured, Pat was unconscious immediately after the storm. The three were lying in the open for a while.

"Someone took $400 out of my husband's pocket, $60 out of my billfold," Kanavy says. She is sure that her son had money. It too vanished.

For some survivors, the constant stream of sightseers took a toll. Floyd and Bonnie McCain in Cowley County felt harassed by the people who constantly drove by their house to look at the damage.

"We got rude and testy," Bonnie says. "We felt like monkeys in a zoo."

For other people, their experiences were simply baffling.

In Wichita, Contreras and Wilson worried about looting. They sent their children to stay with family and friends and took turns napping in the car.

"Around 4 or 5 in the morning, I saw a man walking up to the car. Nobody else was around, and I gripped the butcher knife I was holding a little tighter. He knocked on the window and asked if I was OK, and I said, 'Yes, what do you want?' He asked if he could say a prayer for me. I said, 'Well, yes.' He said a prayer out loud and then he left. He just disappeared down the street."

Forty-eight hours after the tornadoes rumbled out of the survivors lives, their self-preservation frenzy began to pass; their frantic search for belongings was subsiding.

The reality of their new circumstances started to settle uneasily on them. The tasks ahead were many. There was mourning to do — for the dead, for their homes, for their loss of innocent security.

Most were relieved to be alive and have their families at hand. But where were they going to live? How were they going to live? What about their jobs? Would they feel whole again?

People pondered what they had experienced.

For Detective Sherry the tornado is the biggest he had ever seen. For Sgt. See, the resulting disaster, even in a career that deals in life's daily disasters, was of a magnitude that for him was previously unimaginable.

Tony McCrary proclaims, "I don't ever want to be in another one."

For Andover, Wichita, Haysville, Nortonville, Abbyville, Willowbrook, Cowley and Elk counties and all the other places that had suffered through storms in1991,McCrary's statement was a universal prayer. Δ

*"They thought they were picking up souvenirs, but it was looting in my book."*

–Jerald Cale

Carol Hamill, owner of Carol's Kitchen, serves food at the Andover Middle School. After the tornado destroyed her restaurant, Hamill moved her operation to the school and fed residents and vounteers. Photo by Tom Schoening.

Verna Abercrombie was one of the first people on the scene in Andover to help after the tornado struck. Two days later, she was appointed vounteer coordinator of the Andover Recovery Committee. Photo by Janet Majure.

# Andover's Hearts Beat As One

On Friday, April 26, Verna Abercrombie of Andover was one of the first people to rush to the devastated area to offer help. All Friday night and all day Saturday, she worked to do whatever seemed most urgent. By Sunday night, she was in charge. All in all, Abercrombie says, it has been an amazing experience.

The work has been emotionally taxing, says the former teacher who chairs volunteer services for the Andover Recovery Committee.

"The hardest part in helping was seeing the people come in who had been hit and working with them on a one-to-one basis."

The work has also been wild.

On the Sunday morning after the tornado, the relief workers realized they needed can openers. Radio stations broadcast the need.

"We got can openers like you wouldn't believe," Abercrombie says.

Sometimes it was confusing. In fact, the relief workers developed a saying: "Flexibility is the key to all disasters."

"Just when you think you know where to get a hold of people and you know how to do things, it would all change," Abercrombie says.

During its work, the Andover committee served every damaged area, not just Andover. Because no one died in some sections of Wichita, for example, outsiders were not as aware of people's need, she says.

Abercrombie's first job for the committee was to train

with the volunteers from the Mennonite Disaster Service, who were experienced in doing this kind of work.

"I spent the whole (first) week doing what needed to be done, going from the Red Cross to the food bank to clothing. One week later, we were set up."

Some problems the committee faced were expected. Some were not. One of the biggest problems was finding a place for all the clothing, both new and used, that had been donated, she says.

"We had a massive amount of clothing." Clothing had to be stockpiled in churches and gyms.

The clothing bank that supplied people who had lost clothing in the tornado was open for six weeks. After that, the committee was left with eight truckloads of clothing.

Another problem came when school was reopened the week after the tornado. Since the middle school kitchen was being used to feed the homeless, the schools had to serve sack lunches to the children.

Helping people at the food bank was also difficult. Volunteers asked people to sign a list and then they stayed with the people to make certain that they would take what they needed.

"I hurt to see people you know and love in that situation," Abercrombie says. "It was even harder to get them to take what they needed because they would say, 'Other people will need this more than me.'"

One night the superintendent of schools came to the food bank. His home had been destroyed by the

**Left:** The clothing bank at the Andover United Methodist Church is packed with donated clothing. Photo by Tom Schoening.

**Right:** Carol and Caleb Scheve meet with the Red Cross case worker. Their home in Andover was destroyed. Photo b Roger Bain.

tornado.

"I knew it had to be really hard. He's a leader in the community," Abercrombie says.

But, the superintendent's shopping trip was important, Abercrombie says. It made other people feel comfortable about shopping in the food bank.

By August, Abercrombie had shifted her efforts to longer-term needs, such as determining whether victims would have enough cold-weather clothing. She also worked with a group called Trees for Andover, which was co-founded by Karen McCrary. The group is working to replace the hundreds of trees that were destroyed by the tornado. For Abercrombie, the recovery work has been rewarding.

"It has made me realize I probably took my community for granted," she says. "Although I have been active and involved, I have been too complacent. I love my community. I love Andover and you don't take what you love for granted. There were a lot of heroes that came out of this."

The attitude in town was exemplified by another saying coined by the relief workers, Abercrombie says. That saying is: "Andover's hearts beat as one."    Δ

*"It has made me realize I probably took my community for granted."*

–Verna Abercrombie

## THE COST OF MAJOR STORMS – MARCH THROUGH JUNE 1991

| Date – Type of Storm | Location | Deaths | Injuries | Damage |
|---|---|---|---|---|
| **March 26** | | | | |
| Hail | Lawrence | 0 Deaths | 1 Injury | $22.00 million |
| Tornadoes | Reno & Pratt Counties | 0 Deaths | 7 Injuries | $8.20 million |
| Tornadoes | Cowley, Allen Counties, entire state | 0 Deaths | 10 Injuries | $3.00 million |
| **April 10** | | | | |
| High Winds | Western Kansas | 0 Deaths | 0 Injuries | $1.00 million |
| **April 11** | | | | |
| Tornado | Stockton in Rooks County | 0 Deaths | 1 Injury | $1.50 million |
| **April 26** | | | | |
| Tornado | Sedgwick & Butler Counties | 17 Deaths | 302 Injuries | $268.40 million |
| Tornado | Cowley County | 1 Death | 0 Injuries | $5.60 million |
| Tornado | Elk County | 1 Death | 2 Injuries | • |
| Tornado | Jefferson & Atchison Counties | 0 Deaths | 6 Injuries | $0.75 million |
| Tornado | Washington | 0 Deaths | 6 Injuries | • |
| Tornadoes | Montgomery & Greenwood Counties | 0 Deaths | 0 Injuries | $0.55 million |
| **May 16** | | | | |
| Tornado | Sedgwick County | 0 Deaths | 0 Injuries | $1.00 million |
| **May 26** | | | | |
| High Winds | Johnson County | 1 Death | 0 Injuries | • |
| High Winds | Wilson State Park | 0 Deaths | 12 Injuries | • |
| **June 15** | | | | |
| Lightning/Fire | University of Kansas | 0 Deaths | 0 Injuries | $18.0 million |
| **Totals**<br>• No Estimate Available | | 20 Deaths | 347 Injuries | $330.00 million |

From National Weather Service Storm Data and Unusual Weather Phenomena and Kansas Storms 1991 staff reports

Left: At this point in the video Greg Jarrett and Ted Lewis of NewsChannel 3 are trying to outrun the tornado. The funnel is just right of center. Courtesy of NewsChannel 3, Wichita.

As the tornado roars toward the overpass, a car can be seen tumbling in the funnel. The car is the black dot at the right bottom of the tornado. Look at the point where the funnel, which is in the top left of the photo, touches the road. Courtesy of NewChannel 3, Wichita.

# The Video Seen Around The World

The first thing a viewer sees on the video is a huge column of what looks like spiraling white smoke reaching from the ground to a towering black cloud in the sky above. Wisps of white twirl lazily together as the column moves toward the camera. Birds sing heartily. The camera bounces. A man's voice is audible as the camera operator climbs into a station wagon. He points the camera lens out the window. The car moves. At first, it moves slowly.

The man is speaking slowly and calmly. He tells the driver they have plenty of time to view the funnel. Suddenly the man speaks quickly, running his words together as if the sentence was one long word that would urge the driver on.

"Lots faster lots faster Greg. It's catching us. We gotta go buddy. We gotta really go. You gotta blaze, buddy!"

*"Lots faster lots faster Greg. It's catching us. We gotta go buddy."*

–Ted Lewis

The speaker is Ted Lewis, a cameraman for KSNW News Channel 3 in Wichita. The driver is Greg Jarrett, a KSNW reporter. Captured on the video is their flight from an F2-class tornado that is chasing them down the Kansas Turnpike. The winds inside the funnel were swirling at speeds as high as 157 miles per hour.

Minutes before, Lewis and Jarrett had been calm as they drove south toward Wichita after completing a routine assignment in northeastern Kansas. Their conversation had turned to a subject discussed by many reporters. They wondered if they would ever get lucky and be in the right place at the right time to capture an award-winning spot news story. So far, neither had.

It was a little after 7 p.m. near El Dorado on April 26. The first sign of danger was debris falling out of the air. They spotted the tornado and stopped their car. Lewis began shooting the tornado, which was spawned by the same storm cell that produced the funnel that had just ravaged Haysville, Wichita and Andover. In a few minutes, it was clear that the tornado was heading directly at the two men. They climbed in the car and sped away.

For several minutes, the two men played a cat-and-mouse game with the tornado. First they sped off, then stopped to film the funnel when it seemed safe, then they sped off again as the funnel came closer. At one point, they realized that no traffic was coming at them in the northbound lane. Jarrett drove the car across the median and sped north for a while before crossing the median again to head south. The white funnel was gaining on them.

They headed for an overpass known as the Benson

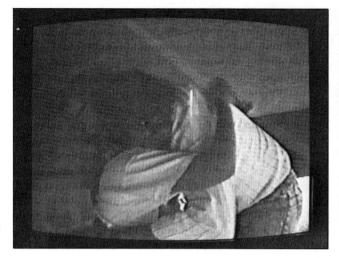

After the tornado passes, survivors embrace under the bridge. Courtesy of News Channel 3, Wichita.

**Right:** The tornado rumbles away from the overpass. Courtesy of Newchannel 3, Wichita.

*"We're not going to make it. . .This is a silly way to die."*

–Greg Jarrett

Bridge, the only shelter they could see. Several other cars were already under the bridge.

As they raced toward the bridge, Jarrett thought, "We're not going to make it...This is a really silly way to die."

Tires squealing, they stopped under the bridge. Carrying his camera, Lewis jumped from the car. Jarrett got out, looked toward the other people and pointed at the underside of the bridge. He can be heard on the video shouting, "Get under the girders." Jarrett says he remembered that two other KSNW reporters had hidden in the girders of another bridge a year before to avoid a tornado.

The two men struggled up the steep hill and wedged their bodies between a concrete slab and the bridge's steel girders. Lewis pointed the camera lens toward the oncoming tornado. It is clearly visible in the tape as a solid white column. Lewis and Jarrett hung on to each other. Lewis clung desperately to the camera.

"The wind was pushing me against the embankment," Lewis says.

On the videotape, a viewer sees square chunks of something black and solid fly through the air as the wind flattens the tall grass. A deep rumbling roar drowns out any other sound, then the tornado has passed. Lewis turned the camera around. The viewer can see the white funnel speed away.

Screams become audible on the tape. After a moment, Jarrett took the microphone and began interviewing the other survivors under the bridge. A girl is seen crying and holding onto her father. Later the two men got back in their car and drove down the turnpike. They taped scenes of tangled trucks and cars and rescuers kneeling over bleeding motorists.

Heading toward Wichita, the two men sped down the turnpike. They were excited. They had finally been in the right place.

By the time they reached their television station, their elation was gone. All the way home, they had heard reports of the devastation of the tornado that had traveled through Haysville, Wichita and Andover.

It was not until the two men had a chance to look at the videotape that they learned it had captured a picture of a van caught in the tornado. The van tumbled like a dark pebble in the white funnel cloud.

That night the station broadcast the video and fed it to NBC and CNN. Both networks interviewed Jarrett and Lewis on camera. The two men did telephone and satellite interviews with reporters from around the world, then they worked for the next two weeks at covering the disaster's aftermath.

Jarrett says he had to numb his feelings during the tornado and immediately afterwards.

"You get into a mindset when you're out covering human tragedy a lot in your career," he says. "You just have to get in the frame of mind, 'I have to do it.'"

Lewis says he did not realize how dangerous the situation had been under the bridge until he saw the face of the terrified girl who was screaming.

Shortly after the tornado, Jarrett moved on to a new job with the Court TV Network as one of its three main anchors. An attorney, Jarrett was hired before the tornado. Lewis continued working for KSNW as a photojournalist. The video was nominated for an Emmy for photography.                     Δ

A wood stove was one of the only things left standing after the tornado swept through Hardy and Stephanie Streeter's house in Cowley County. Photo by Barbara Streeter

Right: Steve Sapp, Ron Stein, Daisy Cox (left to right) sit outside Cox Farms' newly opened market. The business opened in August despite the fact the building was not yet finished.

# Legacy of the Storm

These quotes were collected through interviews and questionnaires about four months after the tornadoes struck Kansas. Some people are quoted more than once.

"I tell you what, the good old Lord is in my heart now. It's changed our life a lot. We don't take anything for granted anymore, and we watch the weather like the back of our hand. We watch it day and night." — Donna Tobler, the Timber Lane section of Haysville

"I just can't even talk about it today. It makes me sick to my stomach. It's with you morning, noon and night. You don't sleep at night. We're just existing, not living." — Helen Stein, part-owner of Cox Farm in Wichita

The day after the tornado ripped through Wichita this was the view into the TV room in Warren and Rosemary Benn's house on East 53rd Street. Photo by Rosemary Benn.

"We still can't think straight. We just go on nerves." — Bonnie McCain, Cowley County

"Nothing will ever be normal again. You think you're safe in your own home but you're not." — Stephanie Streeter, Cowley County

"It consumes our thoughts, plans, energies and all our time. We are both so very weary." — Mildred and George Benson, near Willowbrook

"Recovery is taking a long time. I had nightmares on the 26th of every month."-Rosemary Benn, Wichita

"I don't think there is a day gone by when I haven't thought about April 26 and what impact it has had on my life. During that day, myself and Matt Foster, a student here at KU at the time and also a member of the KU Severe Storms Chase Team, we headed west of Lawrence to intercept the storms...It was an exciting day for myself as I saw my first tornado. However, It was hard to be excited when we later learned about what happened around Wichita. It's difficult to be so fascinated by a force of nature that can kill so many people."-Rodney Price, University of Kansas

"The nightmares will more than likely continue for a while longer." — Karen McCrary, Andover

The tornado roars toward Haysville after hitting Clearwater. Photo by Linda Word.

Right: Homeowners outside of Andover attempt to salvage belongings on April 28 from their house two miles east of Andover Road. Photo by David Bruce Oxley.

*"It was an awful sight and sickening to know that homes were being ripped apart instantly and people were dying as I watched."*

–Marganne Winter Oxley

"My feeling was: How could something so beautiful be so dangerous and destructive? I was standing under clear blue skies and sunshine and just north and east of me was black and deadly looking. It was truly an unforgettable feeling. It seemed huge and unmercifully powerful but I didn't even have a strong wind or rain where I was." —Linda Word, near Haysville

"We live 3 1/2 miles east of Andover in the country. We had a clear view of the tornado. Homes, walls, cars, big debris was swirling skyward. It was an awful sight and a sickening feeling to know that homes were being ripped apart instantly and people were dying as I watched."–Marganne Winter Oxley, Augusta

"The number of shoes that were left in the Golden Spur trailer park, the shoes were everywhere that you looked."–Brett Bohannon, a 17-year old photographer who saw the aftermath of the storm in Andover

"I see Grandma as not being afraid of it even when it was happening because she had such tremendous faith. I just know she was thinking. 'I'm going home.' That's one thing that helps me. To her it was a promotion; she got to be with the Lord.

"That's really the only thing that keeps me with my head above water about it, knowing they got to go together and Grand Dad didn't have to go to a nursing home. All the things he feared were taken care of–in a sense.

"The only fear that I have is that they saw it" — Liz Spencer, talking about Gladys and Robert Manes, who died in Andover

"I personally lost my father...I helped a couple (John and Kay) who lived two trailers east of my Dad. They both had pretty severe injuries. I was the first one there to help both of them. I put my coat over Kay so she wouldn't go into shock. I called Dr. Stephan Lemons, the first doctor there, over to help John and Kay. I went to get anything I could find to keep both of them warm...I thank God that they are OK and for giving me the wisdom and courage to help them.

"I believe that God led me to help them and I was able to give something to them that I couldn't give to my Dad. God has my Dad now and I know he's safe and in God's care. Rest in peace, my beloved Dad." — Teresa Warren, whose father Robert Meininger died in Andover

"I wake up and wonder why I'm here. . . I was thrown 80 feet and the whole house came down on top of me. How did I get out of there?" — Clarence Capps, Wichita

"I wake up at night and have goose bumps. If it had happened two hours later we'd all been dead. We would all been in the house eating dinner. The TV wouldn't have been on." — Felix Lawson, Wichita

"About a week after the tornado, someone came to me and said, 'Julie, I haven't even seen you cry yet. Are you still numb or what?' I said, 'Oh, I cry every night, tears of joy, thanking God for leaving me the one thing that means the most to me, my family." — Julie Maben, Goddard

A refrigerator still stands in Brenda and Danny Welborn's kitchen. Photo by Gloria Harrington.

Right: Friends and relatives attempt to salvage household items from Dale and Julie Maben's trailer, which turned over in one April 26 tornado. Julie and two of her children ran out the front door. Dale and one son ran out the back door, but the 4-year-old was inside when the trailer flipped. The child survived with only a scratch. Photo by Jack Price.

"I've been in a car wash once since the tornado, and I freaked. The sound of the water, the pressure on the windows...I was just shaking when I came out of it." — Cheryl Contreras, Wichita

"We never found the outside walls to our house. We found one little piece about (three inches around). We knew it was part of my kitchen wall because one side had the wallpaper, but as far as the outside walls, we never saw any of our walls." — Charlene Fairman, Andover

"It's sad to see the trees stripped to nothing." — Sharon Andes, Winfield

"The storm destroyed 30 years of work and love we put into our home and grounds. We came through the storm with no physical injuries even though we were in the house at the time, but our hearts are broken by the loss. It's as if we've lost a member of our family. It is like a grieving process. We experienced anger, despair, sorrow and a true sense of loss." — Marsha Callaway, Wichita

"The tornado changed all our lives. As three of us watched it go northeast and down the hill after hitting us, we didn't realize how everything had changed within less than a minute. We no longer had a home, all we had worked for for the last few years was gone. There are a lot of things to do and decisions to make that you didn't realize you'd have to make such as where are you going to live. Are you going to live in a mobile home again?" —

Brenda Welborn, Meriden

"Immediately after seeing our beloved home so violated I began to shake in a way I didn't know possible. I felt loss as quickly as I would have had it been one of our children. It was not just wood and glass and plaster that was destroyed, it was our home, so many memories and dreams lived there." –Juna Keever, Hutchinson

"Was this a judgment of God? Why us? What had we done to deserve this? I never once blamed God." — Mildred Benson, near Willowbrook

"I live daily, since the April 26, 1991, tornado, watching the sky and listening to the weather alert radio station for severe weather. It's difficult for me to relax, sleep and work my job." — Loretta Shaffstall, Andover

"Emotionally I have tended to be very cranky and irritable very easily. Spiritually, I thank God every day for my life as well as my wife, daughter and friends. I feel that this event has brought me even closer to God." — Tony McCrary Andover

Four months after the tornado, Linda Levernez' children told her they wanted to move from the home on Minnie Street in Wichita where they had hidden from the tornado. Linda said, "This is our house. This is where we're going to live!"

"I guess I'll rebuild. My heart's not in it." — Gereda Edwards, between Andover and Towanda

A crib and fragments are all that survived the destruction of Julie and Dale Maben's trailer. Photo by Judy Boschmann.

Loretta Shaffstall (center) sits in front of the rubble that was once her house in the Golden Spur Mobile Home Park. Photo by LaVeda Horst.

Right: Neighbors sort through the wreckage of Don Snyder's shop building at his home near Burden. Photo by Ed Redfield.

*"I have always believed in and respected Mother Nature. Don't know why anyone would live in Kansas without a basement."*

–Robert Dolan

"We were one of the first ones who decided to build back (in the same place)." — Gloria Capps, Wichita "We were still in shock." — Clarence Capps, Gloria's husband

"I have always believed in and respected Mother Nature. Don't know why anyone would live in Kansas without a basement." — Robert Dolan, Wabaunsee County

"People said, 'Didn't you have nightmares?' I said, 'No, I didn't have any nightmares. It happened. We're through. We're here...The only thing I'd have nightmares about is if I had no insurance and had to pay for all of it." — Gloria Capps, Wichita

"Instead of counting sheep when I can't sleep, I arrange furniture in our new home." — Mildred Benson, near Willowbrook

"It's given us an opportunity to get a home ... A real house, that's what I call them, a house without wheels." – Liz Spencer, Andover, talking about the tornado and the resulting insurance money they got for the loss of their mobile home

"We celebrated our 62nd anniversary this past June. We now have the roof back on the house and drain pipes up and windows in, also steps on the front porch. Outside, the car shed is back on its foundation and has a new roof. We had to completely build the north hay barn back and we got it done in time for this years hay crop. The fences are mostly down yet. We did get a corral fence built back in time to wean this year's calf crop. We are still cutting up downed trees, picking up sticks and rocks. There is a lot to do yet.

"Many times (before the tornado) we were told what a pretty place we had. Due to the many cedar trees, I think. The west shelter, gone now, were cedars. The north shelter grove was mostly walnut with hedge on the east side. It's gone now also. The loss of our trees hurt the most as we'll never live to see others take their place." –Leona, 81, and Don Snyder,84, Burden

"Miraculously, no one was at home at the time the tornado wiped out our entire two-story ranch house, garage, barns, stock trailers, everything–destroyed. The feeling we had when we drove back 'home' and found our yard filled with so many friends and neighbors is one we cannot describe even now. We were truly blessed by not only no one being at home, but by everything that everyone did for weeks after the tornado. The support was unbelievable. Roger's family in South Dakota even hosted a 'Gone with the Wind' shower for us!" –Linda and Roger Bartel, Cambridge

"The storm just reinforced my conviction that people are all basically good and care for each other, especially in a disaster." — Kenny Weishaar, Nortonville fire chief

"It has changed my view of things and people, both good and bad. Sightseers make you feel naked. Friends and family who cry with you and help you to try and recover are priceless. Pickup trucks at 11:30 p.m. driving around are trouble. Some insurance companies are not

About 1/4 mile from where Roger and Linda Bartel's home once stood, friends relatives and neighbors search through the debris of their house. Wreckage was strewn for miles. Photo by Linda Bartel.

Right: Donald Thomas puts the finishing touches on the graffitti he sprayed on his house in Haysville. Photo by Derrick Vogt.

concerned about their customers as much as they are the company.'' — Marsha Callaway, Wichita

"I don't think it changed me any. I was praying before the storm and I was praying after it.'' — Ann Huss, Nortonville

"I think the one thing that passes through my mind most frequently is the admonition of an old Swedish Lutheran pastor I once knew: 'Don't store up treasures on Earth.'" — Tollie Hartmann, Andover

"The storm has certainly made me realize that material things are not the most important things in my life...The storm has brought me closer in my walk with God.'' — Kathleen Long, Andover

"The storm has changed my view of life. In a matter of minutes, families lost priceless family treasures, but no one lost his life.'' — Pat Donohue, Willowbrook

"We felt we were safe with a basement, but nothing was left covering the basement. There was much debris in the basement. I believe it was God that made sure my family and I were at a restaurant in town at the time of the storm." -Jim Keever, Jr. Hutchinson

"I feel the Lord spared me for some reason, and I wonder what direction he will lead me now. I must make a difference!'' — Barbara Pearce, Wichita

"Life is so short and full of thorns. Make the best of it.

Make lemonade from lemons.'' — Donald Thomas, Haysville

"We are Mennonites and believe very strongly in God. These storms show us a small part of the very awesome power of God. We know we are not promised tomorrow. These storms that form and roll across the Kansas prairies, as long as they don't hurt anyone can be very beautiful and powerful. They are the things that man cannot change or control. Our destiny lies in the hands of God.'' — Susan Brewer, Potwin

"We don't worry so much about little things anymore. Financially, we are sinking, but emotionally we are very stable.'' — Dawn Pampel, Wichita

"Rather than a tragic situation, I feel very fortunate. We were left with those things that matter most, our lives and health.'' — Lanell Mauzey, Atchison County

"One night after cleaning up...my boys built a bonfire in the drive and sat there past midnight with 'remember when' stories. It's similar to when their Dad died. We have our memories but it's a chapter closed.'' — Dorothy Fox, 65, Wichita, talking about her sons aged 26 to 40

"Storms do happen. They disrupt lives. Sometimes you just have to take your turn.'' — Wilma Anglemyer, Winfield

"God does not promise to keep his children from trials, but does promise to go through them with us and to not give us more than we can bear. You wonder about that truth when you don't know where to start,

*"I feel the Lord spared me for some reason, and I wonder what direction he will lead me now. I must make a difference!"*

–Barbara Pearce

One hour after the tornado struck Ron and Dawn Pampel's home in Wichita, Dawn took this picture of the back of their house.

Right: Scott Anglemyer (right) and his cousin, Cowley County Sheriff's Deputy Rick Eastman (left) look into the basement of the home of Scott's parents, Arlan and Wilma Anglemyer near Winfield. Photo by Katie Eastman.

which of 25 decisions you should attempt first, when you don't have anything to cut your toe nails with and you realize you have to buy something to use as rags! Then, he gives inward peace, smooths things out and gives a sense of humor." — Betty Parks, Andover

"We love the Lord, we love Kansas and we still love our little corner on Highway 160 east of Winfield." — Wilma Anglemyer, Winfield. Δ

> *"We love the Lord, love Kansas and we still love our little corner on Highway 160 east of Winfield."*
>
> –Wilma Anglemyer

# On Finding To-Do Lists in the Tornado Rubble

Picking up Legos and kindergarten papers as a Mennonite Disaster Service volunteer in Andover didn't seem so different from what I do at home. Only this home a was entirely sky-lit, and pieces of insulation and broken glass added to the clutter in the little boy's room.

Then I went to the kitchen where the stove and dishwasher were overturned, though some cupboards and drawers were still good. I looked for things I would want saved if this were my house. Among them I found two to-do lists.

These were not scribbled reminders on backs of used envelopes like mine, but specific items written neatly on notebook papers, stapled together to make a wider paper. I read the outdoor jobs:

- Tighten up fence
- Clean garage
- Sweep sidewalks, rake yard
- Remove sand pile
- Pick up trash

And I thought:
(Tighten up fence) What fence?
(Clean garage) No garage left, either.
(Sweep sidewalks, rake yard) Bulldoze them first.
(Remove sand pile) All done for you.
(Pick up trash) Still needs doing, now more than ever.

The Price family, whose 'to-do's' I was reading, were all spared in the tornado. They would have more 'to-do' lists in their new home.

We too, as well as our house, were spared when the tornado hit Hesston in 1990. I thought of the lines of a poem, 'Everything done on Earth will pass; Only what's done for Christ will last.'

How true.

Our houses do look better when the windows are washed and the sidewalks are swept, but a tornado can un-do all our work on these things in a minute. Only what's done for Christ–for people–will last.
–by Susan Balzer  Δ

The merchants of Andover Square shopping center are open for business as the Center is rebuilt around them. Photo by Stan Thiessen.

Carol Hamill stands outside her new restaurant, which opened Sept. 27, 1991. Shortly after the tornado destroyed her business, Hamill was severly injured in a car accident. "I think my guardian angel lives on Rolaids." Hamill says.

# Rebuilding Lives

The struggle to rebuild can take months or even years. When contacted in mid-summer about four months after the tornado struck, survivors talked about the emotional and financial cost of the struggle. They talked about new friends they had made, and the loved ones they would never see again. They talked about the birth of new hopes and the loss of old dreams. What follows is a recounting of their stories. The survivors are listed in alphabetical order under the name of their home town or county.

*"It was getting to the point where I could lay back and now I've got to start all over again."*

*–Gereda Edwards*

## Andover

**Gereda Edwards,** between Andover and Towanda, stayed with relatives immediately after the tornado destroyed her dream home.

Later friends offered their mobile home. The friends are truck drivers who are out of town most of the time, Edwards says.

"She said, 'You know where the key is.' She said, 'You can stay there at that mobile home as long as you want to,' so that's where I've been staying."

Edwards says she supposes that she will rebuild, but admits that her heart is not in the project.

"It's a lot of work and a lot of headaches," Edwards says.

Rebuilding seems even more difficult since the house the tornado destroyed had just been built.

"It was getting to the point where I could lay back and now I've got to start all over again," Edwards says.

**Jim, Charlene, Jimmy Fairman,** Golden Spur, continued to struggle with problems of finding a new home and a new job for Charlene. Charlene's job as a waitress at Livingston's Restaurant was blown away when the tornado destroyed the restaurant.

Immediately after the storm, the family stayed in motels. Later, they rented an apartment in Wichita. Insurance did not completely cover their loss. Despite a housing grant from the Federal Emergency Management Agency, the family still did not have enough money to buy a house. Instead, they planned to buy a mobile home by fall and move back into Golden Spur. Remaining in Andover will allow Jimmy to continue attending Andover Middle School, but the family's decision to remain is based on more than that.

"We want to be in Andover," Charlene says. "It's home. We looked at a lot of places, but they didn't look right. They didn't make you feel comfortable."

**Tollie Hartmann,** an electrical engineer, Countryside Third Addition, has been able to repair her house. Her

Little remained of the Kiser house on Douglas. This photo was taken on the day after the tornado. Photo by Janet Kiser.

Right: A tree uprooted by the tornado lies in a field northeast of Andover. Photo by Janet Majure.

*"I've got a lot to do, a lot more than I ever have had in my life."*

–Janet Kiser

home was the only home in her neighborhood to survive the storm. The family moved back into the home in mid-August.

**Brook Ibarra** was recovering from the injuries she suffered when she was caught outside as the tornado rolled out of Andover and churned over the countryside north of town.

The broken bones have mended, but Ibarra says it will take time before she is psychologically and financially back in shape.

"I've been other places when storms came up and I was OK," Ibarra says. "But here at home, when a cloud comes up, I freak. It even bothers me when a jet goes over."

Money has also been a struggle. Ibarra did not qualify for government assistance because her home was not destroyed. However, her car was totaled, and her injuries kept her out of work. Ibarra did carry health insurance, but the deductible plus the co-payment policy left her with large hospital bills.

**Pat Kanavy** was seriously injured in the tornado that killed her husband and son near Golden Spur. The family was driving near the mobile home park when the tornado struck.

Kanavy says she has almost recovered physically, although problems remain.

"Can't smell, can't taste, " she says. "It's real hard to breathe through my nose."

Kanavy says she is not ready to talk about what happened. She has blacked out everything that happened from Friday when the tornado struck to the Sunday afterward.

**Janet, Kelly, Katy and Kyle Kiser** stayed with Janet's family immediately after the tornado destroyed their home on Douglas Street. They rented an apartment in Wichita before buying and moving into a new house in Andover.

"We did not feel we could rebuild at this time and make the decisions we would have to make," Janet says. "We loved that home. We knew we could have a nice house back, but not that house. We couldn't have made the decisions."

Janet says the family handled the disaster well, in part because of her husband's insistance that material things were not important.

"My kids never did ask for anything," Janet says. The family is pleased to have a home again, she says.

"I've got a lot to do, a lot more than I ever have had in my life."

**Russ Griffith**, co-owner of the company that operates Green Valley Greens Golf Course, Andover's municipal course, has been hard at work fixing the damage the tornado inflicted on the course.

"We're a long ways from being cleaned up after that," he says. "We have done the essentials.

"This course is kind of a pasture turning into a monument of golfing play," he says with a small chuckle.

The tornado delayed the company's efforts to perfect the golf course.

"It doesn't look nearly as attractive because of all the fallen trees," he says.

Griffith hopes to be able to tap into some of the money Andover has received to repair its recreational facilities.

Loretta Shaffstall's new mobile home on Rhondda was the first replacement home to be placed in Golden Spur Mobile Home Park. Photo by Kevin Shaffstall.

A salvaged foundation ready for rebuilding in Countryside Third Addition in Andover. In the background are the new mobile homes in Golden Spur. Photo by Stan Thiessen.

Months after the tornado, the funnel's path was still easily identifiable where rows of trees are interrupted by barren spaces. Twisted trees stand at the edges of the gaps.

**Kathleen Long**, Golden Spur, has not yet been able to find a permanent home. The mobile home she lived in for nine years was destroyed in the tornado.

Immediately afterwards, she stayed with her son in an apartment, but her long-term plans were uncertain. Long says she would love to have another mobile home, but she fears she can't afford it.

Long had little equity in her home or car. She has no money left to start over. The situation seems particularly onerous to her because she is 53, Long says.

"I can hardly stand the thought of going $50,000 in debt," she says.

After the tornado, Long found nothing but fragments of her former home. Later, items appeared in the mail that people had found miles away. The items evidently contained enough identification for people to mail them to her. Since the tornado, Long says she has been more cautious.

**Betty Parks**, Golden Spur, had lived in the park for five years. She has relocated to another mobile home park.

Parks misses family pictures and the things her children had made, but she says she is thankful.

"Really, what the Lord has given me back is nicer," Parks says. "I have bought another mobile home. I did buy a weather alert radio. There's a shelter where I am. I am not fearful; I wasn't before. I hope I will be more cautious."

Immediately after the tornado, her family was frantic to find her because of a mixup about where Parks had sought shelter. Parks says she learned something as a result of their concern.

"It really helped cement their feelings for me, and it was good to see the grandkids would have missed me so much. There are seven of those."

**Tony and Karen McCrary**, Golden Spur, were able to move back into Golden Spur after the tornado. They have a new mobile home. Karen is a founder of Trees for Andover.

**Steve, Patricia, Angie, Shad Rockstad** moved into a house of a friend immediately after the tornado and stayed for months before moving into a duplex built on the same spot as the duplex destroyed by the tornado. The family had lived in the home for only two years before it was destroyed.

"The landlord rebuilt it, so it was new for a second time," he says.

The new duplex is basically the same design built onto the same foundation. That made moving back feel a bit strange.

"It's exactly the same," Steve says. "The dog and cat acted like they were just glad to be home."

**Allen Sargent**, Golden Spur, lost his wife Katherine in the tornado. Sargent, his daughter Michelle Sargent and his wife's daughter Kristina Kinyon were all injured.

*"There's a shelter where I am. I am not fearful; I wasn't before. I hope I will be more cautious."*

*–Betty Parks*

At his new home, Keith Harpstrite unloads a trailer of items salvaged from his destroyed home near Andover. Photo by Stan Thiessen.

New construction and rubble stand side by side in an Andover housing development where scores of homes were destroyed. Photo by Janet Majure.

The See family (left to right) Paul Troy, Matthew, Roseanna, Elijah and Elizabeth at their temporary home in Wichita. Their home in Andover's Golden Spur Mobile Home Park was destroyed.

Sargent expected to return to work in September after spending 13 days in the hospital and recuperating at home. He suffered cuts in his leg, a severe glass cut above the elbow in the nerves of his right arm and an 18-inch-long cut in his left buttock that took four months to heal.

A structural draftsman at Boeing, Sargent hopes that his right arm will work well enough to allow him to draft manually. If not, he says he can use a computer.

"The girls are recovering pretty well," Sargent says. Kristina suffered a broken arm and a "blow-out fracture" of her eye, Long says. This kind of fracture occurs when the bone around the eye is broken and puts pressure on the soft eye tissue. Doctors reconstructed the socket, Sargent says. Kristina spent 11 days in the hospital.

Michelle had a piece of 2 X 4 lumber in her lung and broken ribs. Her jaw was broken in three places and she suffered bruises, cuts and scrapes. Michelle stayed in the hospital for 13 days..

"She seems to be recovering," Sargent says. "Everybody's doing pretty good physically."

Sargent bought a house in a development south of Golden Spur. He wanted to stay in the Andover School District so that Kristina, who was 13, could continue to go to school there. However, Kristina's father insisted that she move to Texas where she was living with her sister.

Sargent rues the tornado as ending the happiest time in his life. One year before the storm struck, he met Katherine. Nine months before it struck, they were married.

"I couldn't have been any happier. I am so grateful for those nine months."

**Andover Sgt. Paul Troy See, and his wife Roseanna and children Elizabeth, Elijah and Matthew,** Golden Spur, spent the first few days after the tornado with friends and family and then moved into the Holiday Inn.

"We didn't have anywhere to go," See says.

Help came from a couple who saw See talking to reporters on television. The couple, Bill and Mary Belle Ahsmuhs, called the Police Department and asked him if he and his family would like to house sit at their Wichita home for the summer. The Ashmuhses did not charge rent.

"They didn't know us," See says. "We came in Sunday, and they left Tuesday morning. They turned everything over to us."

Since the tornado, the Sees have been struggling financially. The family income fell $350 a month because Troy could not keep his part-time job maintaining a car wash and Roseanna lost some of her child-care work. To make matters worse, the couple did not have enough insurance to cover their financial loss.

"I know we can't afford to buy a house," he says. "So it's either buy another mobile home or rent."

See says it is important to find a place where the family can "go down the stairs into the basement."

After the Ahsmuhses returned to their home in the fall, the Sees planned to move into an apartment to give them time to make a final decision on housing.

Despite the difficulties, See says he and his family feel blessed.

"We came out of this in good shape compared to

Andover rebuilds. Construction nears completion (left) four months after the tornado in the Countryside Third Addition across from the Golden Spur Mobile Home Park. Photo by Stan Thiessen.

Right: Two months earlier (right) building was just beginning on Second Street. Photo by Tom Schoening.

most people," he says.

In August, See and another police officer were honored for their efforts to save Andover.

**Dan Sharshel**, an off-duty EMT who was one of the first medical personnel on the scene in Andover, faced an angry wife immediately after the storm. She was upset because he did not contact her until four hours after the tornado struck. Sharshel's house received minor damage. He felt grateful, though, that he had the training to help people in need.

**Mary Lou Spencer and her daughter-in-law Liz Spencer**, Golden Spur, and the entire Spencer family continued to struggle with two crushing blows inflicted by the tornado: They lost loved ones, and their homes had been destroyed.

For Mary Lou the aftermath was particularly difficult. Her parents, Gladys and Robert Manes, were killed and her close friend Ruby Crawford died trying to get the Manes to shelter. Crawford went on that errand at the request of Mary Lou, who telephoned from work to ask Crawford to help her parents. Also killed in the tornado was Crawford's companion Joe Bobbitt.

The deaths of Bobbitt and Crawford robbed Mary Lou of some of her best friends. Both had played important roles in her life when her husband had died in June 1990.

"When Chuck passed away, they were like Mom and Dad to me," Mary Lou says. "If I needed anything, I would just call them and they would be there."

Months after the tornado struck, the struggle for housing was still not resolved.

"People think that we're set," Mary Lou says. "Everybody thinks we're taken care of."

Liz and her husband have been looking for a house or a lot in Andover, but so far they have had no luck. Both Liz and her family and Mary Lou continued to live with relatives.

Both say they want to stay in Andover. Mary Lou would like to move back into Golden Spur, but utilities had not yet been re-installed in all sections of the park. Despite the delays, Mary Lou has rejected friends' suggestions that she move to nearby Wichita.

"Out here, I know people," Mary Lou says. "It's home; it's still home. If I went to Wichita, I wouldn't know anybody."

**Suzie Storrer**, Douglas Street, and her family lived in El Dorado in the house of friends for about six weeks after the tornado. Later they rented a house in Andover.

Her husband, a builder since 1968, reconstructed their house on the old foundation. The Storrers expected to move into their new home by the end of September whether or not the new home was done.

Moving at that time would mean breaking a one-year lease they were forced to sign in order to rent a house. Storrer says she is disgusted that a one-year lease would be required in Andover in the aftermath of the tornado. Despite the lease, however, it is time to move, she says. "I just want to be home."

The process of rebuilding the house has been interesting. Working at the site four months after the tornado, Suzie found a baby ring. Suzie says she finds

*"When Chuck passed away they were like Mom and Dad to me."*

–May Lou Spencer

Lee Kelly of Winfield stands in front of a tree that was uprooted by the April 26 tornado.

herself having a new perspective to house building. She wants to put her clothes in the basement to protect them and she has questioned her husband about the wisdom of using pink insulation.

"I said, 'Do we have to use this pink insulation? It's such a mess to clean up."

The Storrers and their new friends and benefactors, Duane and Rhonda Neussen, continued to keep in touch. The Neussens were strangers until they showed up shortly after the tornado to help. At first the Neussens did not even tell the Storrers their names.

"Finally, we became good friends," Suzie says. "We spent the Fourth of July with them."

Every time the Storrers get together with their friends, the Neussens give them something new, Suzie says.

"We have been adopted!"

> *"I just want to be home."*
>
> –Suzie Storrer

**Teresa Warren**, daughter of victim Robert Meininger, continued to deal with the emotional aftermath of her father's death.

Teresa, her husband and three children were with her father just before the tornado struck. They intended to eat pizza for dinner. Her stepmother, Nancy, found the body.

People keep telling her to "just forget it," Teresa says. But Teresa says that is not possible yet. "I guess when you get that close to somebody it hurts more."

The way her father died made "forgetting" even more difficult, she says.

Teresa's middle child, now 5, also has had difficulty handling the tornado. He was particularly upset that he never got a chance to have pizza with his grandfather, Teresa says. Δ

# Cowley County

**Donna and Marten Morgan**, spent the night at Marten's boss' house after the tornado leveled their home.

"We stayed up until 3 a.m. talking about it," Donna says.

The Morgans built a new house on the site of their old home. By August, the house had been completed, except for the wallpaper. Next spring they plan to replace the livestock that was lost.

**Hardy, Stephanie and Robert Streeter**, rented a house in Winfield and made plans to rebuild on the site of their original home. They hoped to complete the work within the next five years.

Robert, 7, appeared to have suffered no lasting effects from his harrowing airborne ride, Stephanie says. But she worries that he might have problems later. At the moment, he is bothered when a nearby General Electric plant that builds jet engines fires up the engines for a test, she says.

All three family members were undergoing counseling.

A crane finishes the demolition work that the tornado started on Sam and Helen Tolles' house near Arkansas City. Photo by Patti Morgan.

Bill McKenzie looks through the belongings that he and Aline McKenzie were able to salvage from their home. Photo by Buzz Shaddy.

**Sam and Helen Tolles**, spent the first month after the tornado with their daughter in Arkansas City. They eventually rented a house in town.

Although Sam had retired from his work on the farm before the tornado struck, adjusting to city life has been difficult.

"We're in the process of coming to grips with it," Helen says. Δ

# Elk County

**Richard Jacobs** spent 10 days in the hospital after the tornado killed his wife and destroyed his home. A severely cut leg required many stitches to heal.

Jacobs has moved into a house in Severy. He will not rebuild on the site of his old home. Jacobs says he is still amazed at the fact that he sustained so few injuries in the storm. Jacobs is surrounded by family and old friends.

**Olga Jenkins** spent five weeks in the hospital following the tornado. She suffered four broken ribs, a punctured lung, broken collar bone and broken shoulder blades.

After she left the hospital, Jenkins lived with her daughter, Viola Herndon, in Springfield, Mo. What was left of her farm was pushed into piles of rubble. Jenkins will not return to live there, Herndon says.

"She's been through quite an ordeal," Herndon says. "We're in the process of finding her an apartment."

**Aline and Bill McKenzie** spent the first two weeks after the tornado in a motel in Eureka. Later they moved a large trailer to the site of their house and began to rebuild.

One of the first struggles after the tornado was to calm down and sleep.

"My mind wouldn't settle down on any one thing," Aline says. "You don't sleep much. My mind kept pouring over things and I'd wake up every few hours."

The McKenzies have been rebuilding with the help of Mission, an Oklahoma City organization affiliated with the Methodist church, Aline says. Every week a new crew of volunteers came buy to complete another step in the construction process. Among the additions to the new house was a full basement with a secure storm area, including concrete on the floor, walls and ceiling.

"This time I have a hidy-hole," Aline says.

**Jim Wunderlich and granddaughter Christy Wells** were both doing well. Jim and his wife were working on repairing the damage to their house.

"The thing leaks like a sieve," Wunderlich says. "All we have in there now is a bed, a chair and a TV."

Wunderlich and his wife own a cafe in Piedmont, and Jim operates heavy equipment.

*"You don't sleep much. My mind kept pouring over things and I'd wake up every few hours."*

–Aline McKenzie

Volunteers gather at a Mennonite Disaster Service bus in Andover and wait for instructions before starting their clean-up work. Photo by Susan Balzer.

# Haysville

**Linda Lunsford and her family**, Timber Lane, praise the help of the many recovery organizations that rushed to help after the tornado.

The Mennonite Disaster Service, Red Cross, Salvation Army, the National Guard and broad assortment of friends and strangers provided invaluable services. Some agencies helped people pay bills or buy supplies to make temporary repairs. Others assisted in finding housing for those whose homes had been destroyed.

The storm left the neighborhood with a close feeling it had not had before disaster struck, Linda says.

"Now, you know more of them — stop and chat, trade insurance stories," she says.

The family rented an apartment for part of the siege, then moved in to makeshift quarters in the house before construction workers finished. The Lunsford home was almost completely restored by mid-August.

"I hear people say, 'Oh, I hope it gets me next year,' Linda says. "And I say, 'Oh, no you don't. It's not worth it.' "

**Donna and Tony Tobler**, Timber Lane Addition, stayed in their heavily damaged house while construction crews worked on repairs estimated to cost $34,000. A few weeks after the tornado, before the new roof could be laid, heavy rains poured water into the kitchen and living room. They swept out the rain and started again.

Donna says she sometimes felt depressed and angry because the storm had forced her to live in a partially finished house for three months. Mixed in with her anger was guilt.

"I kind of felt guilty for a long time," she says. "I looked down the neighborhood and saw all those people who had lost their homes. I really hurt inside, wondering where our neighbors were. They just had to get their things and leave."

The Toblers helped deliver boxes of food and clothing to less fortunate neighbors.

Her four children stayed with friends for a few days, until utilities were restored, then returned to stay in the remains of their house.

The tornado did offer the Toblers one advantage. They had been leasing their home with the option to buy. Because of the disaster, they became eligible for a low-cost loan and were able to buy their house. Δ

> *"Now, you know more of them – stop and chat, trade insurance stories."*
>
> –Linda Lunsford

# Jefferson & Atchison Counties

**Joe and Deloris Bonnel** did not have enough insurance to cover their loss. By summer, they had rebuilt a barn. They were waiting for approval of a loan to start rebuilding the house. Mother and son were living

The remains of a tree fill Joe and Judy Keirnses' front yard in Nortonville. Photo by Ken Weishaar.

Debris is scattered through the yard at the Mauzeys. Note that the roof of their house is missing. Photo by Steve Mauzey.

**Joe and Judy Keirns** sold their house to a salvage company after their insurance company declared it to be a total financial loss.

"They jacked it up on beams and cut it in half and left it on the lot for two months," Judy says. "They've moved it to a site where somebody has poured a foundation, and it will be rebuilt."

Immediately after the tornado, the family of five stayed with Joe's parents. Shortly afterwards they received a telephone call from an elderly woman who owned a farmhouse and wanted the family to move in. The woman told the Keirns that she knew they would take care of it.

The family has received enormous help from the community, Judy says. Money has been sent to them anonymously through the mail. The church has given them donations.

"It's overwhelming," Judy says. "What would we do without friends? What would you do if you lived in a bigger community? It's something I'll never forget."

The Keirns continued to rent the farm house in the country five minutes from Nortonville and look for a place to build a new house.

**Steve, Lanell, Arlene and Ginger Mauzey** moved into a rebuilt home on Aug. 29. They had constructed their new house on the same spot as the home that was destroyed by the tornado.

"The whole thing was torn down to the foundation and the stuff stored," Lanell says. A tractor-trailer in their driveway served as storage. At one point all of their possessions were packed in paper bags and stored in the truck.

Immediately after the storm passed, the family found themselves surrounded by help, including two strangers who brought a generator to power lights so the family could work into the night. The next day 20 to 30 people showed up to help.

"I couldn't repay them," Lanell says. "The amount of help we got was unbelievable."

For Lanell there was one loss that would never be restored. Her wedding ring vanished in the tornado. Before the storm, she had placed it on a necklace tree on her dresser.

**Louise Noll's** house received the greatest damage in Nortonville. The first night she stayed with a friend. The next day, her son and daughter arrived from Colorado to help her with the cleanup.

Noll stayed with her sister-in-law Rachael Rauth until she moved to Colorado on June 1.

**Rachael Rauth** made it onto CNN in an interview with a reporter after the tornado.

**Danny and Brenda Welborn** and family in Meriden spent the first few weeks after the tornado dealing with injuries and trips to the hospital.

Danny was hospitalized for two weeks in Topeka with a broken hip and cracked vertebra. Brenda and the boys were also taken to the hospital. She was treated for a broken wrist. Lance required 12 stitches to close a gash

*"I couldn't repay them. The amount of help we got was unbelievable."*

–Lanell Mauzey

with Deloris' sister in Cummings.

101

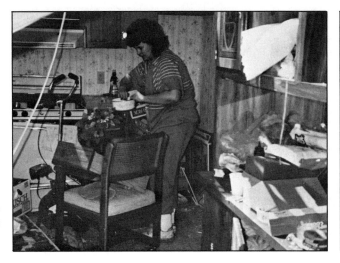

A friend of the Welborns searches their kitchen for salvagable items. Photo by Gloria Harrington.

Four months after the tornado, the site of the McConnell Air Force Base Hospital is a barren field of dirt. Photo by Carol Duerksen.

*"This is my second experience with a tornado. I don't want another."*

–Harriet Whitaker

in his left knee and cuts in his head.

Although Danny has returned to light duties at work, it will be three to five years before he knows whether he will need hip replacement surgery.

The tornado destroyed the family's mobile home. Since the storm, the Welborns have been living in a friend's basement southeast of Meriden. They hope to buy land to build a new home.

Several weeks after the tornado, one of the Welborns' sons found a dresser in a nearby creek. Thinking it might be theirs, Danny went to look at it. It wasn't. The dresser was filled with clothes. The Welborns have yet to learn where the dresser came from.

**Harriet Whitaker** sought shelter at O'Trimbles Funeral Home immediately after the twister struck. Owner Bill O'Trimble had opened his business as a shelter to homeless residents.

O'Trimble's son took Harriet to the emergency room of a hospital in nearby Winchester to have the cut on her arm checked. It took five stitches to close the wound. Whitaker says she really doesn't know how she received the cut.

"This is my second experience with a tornado," she says. "I don't want a third."Δ

## McConnell Air Force Base

Once the tornado left, the base community launched its recovery effort.

"Everyone knew there was work to be done and they did it," says Sgt. Larry Dean of base public affairs. "People put in long shifts doing what needed to be done."

Victim assistance came from the Red Cross, FEMA and the base's own Family Support Center.

"We had people calling and offering us space for the families who lost their homes," Dean says. "Motels offered rooms and many people stayed with friends and family members."

Much of the rebuilding on the base is awaiting bids from contractors. By early 1992, all of the reconstruction is expected to be in progress.Δ

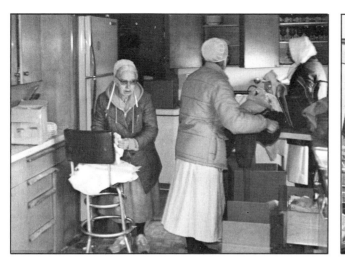

Mennonite Disaster Service volunteers pack up the kitchen at the home of R.E. Wiley in Willowbrook. Photo by Bob Boyd.

Jim Keever Sr. (left) looks through the remains of his son's house. The tornado sheered away two walls and the house collapsed. The second-story bedroom ended up on the first floor. Photo by Jim Keever Jr.

# Pratt & Reno Counties

**Howard J. "Jake" Carey and his family**, Willowbrook, moved into a condominium in Hutchinson immediately after the tornado struck. Their house is in the process of being repaired. The Careys say they spend much of their time at the building site.

"It's as if we're drawn to it," Carey says. "We just have to drive out and check on the progress."

The couple expected to be able to move back into their home in the fall. One of their greatest losses was the 37 trees destroyed around their house. "It's just barren now," Carey says.

**Carol and Ron Heironimus and family**, west of Hutchinson, were recovering from their injuries. Family and friends in the community provided invaluable support, Carol says. But she is disappointed that they had to fight for what the family considered to be fair insurance settlements.

Because the foundation of the house survived, the family was rebuilding on the same spot as their original home. They expected to move into the new house in September.

**Jeremy Lanning and his uncle Mike Lanning,** rural Abbyville, survived the tornado in the basement of Jeremy's grandparents farm house. The house of grandparents Ed and Lena Rush was destroyed, and

there was severe damage to their farm. All five of Jeremy's dogs were found alive and well after the tornado.

The Mennonite Disaster Service helped the Rushes locate about 200 hogs that had been swept away and begin rebuilding. The new house should be finished in the fall.

Jeremy has come to treasure the photograph that Hutchinson News photographer Don Shreve took as he ran from the heap of rubble that had been his home.

**Allan and Sharon Moore,** rural Abbyville, moved in with a son while they rebuilt their farmouse on the original foundation. The new house is smaller, but complete. Construction and the other costs of rebuilding greatly exceeded the money the couple received from their insurance, but it was the loss of 75 trees, some more than a century old, that hurt the most, Sharon says.

**Bob and Donna Schlenz,** rural Preston, moved into another trailer house. Bob is slowly restoring the old farmhouse on their land. Including their damaged trailer, farm buildings and machinery, the tornado did about $100,000 damage to their farm.

**Hutchinson News Photographer Don Shreve** won the Clip of the Month Contest of the National Press Photographers Association for the photograph he took of Jeremy Lanning. The picture appeared in newspapers across the country. ∆

*"It's as if we're drawn to it. We just have to drive out and check on the progress."*

–Jake Carey

On April 27, Gloria and Clarence Cappses' home is in pieces. Photo by Clarence Capps.

Right: On Aug. 7, the Cappses have completed reconstruction of their house. They were one of the first people to rebuild in their Wichita neighborhhood. Photo by Clarence Capps.

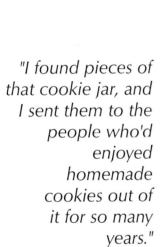

*"I found pieces of that cookie jar, and I sent them to the people who'd enjoyed homemade cookies out of it for so many years."*

–Paula Bruce

# Wichita

**Paula and Herb Bruce**, near 143rd and Kellogg, lived in a mobile home on their land while rebuilding. They expected to move into their new home by fall.

When the tornado swept through the Bruces' home, a ceramic, pineapple-shaped cookie jar that had stored homemade cookies for 24 years was shattered. The jar was an important, treasured part of Paula's kitchen. Before the storm it did not have a chip in it. Afterwards, Paula decided to do something more with the remains than sweep them up and throw them away.

"I found pieces of that cookie jar, and I sent them to the people who'd enjoyed homemade cookies out of it for so many years," she says.

**Marsha and Noble Callaway**, near Pawnee and Greenwich, had built their old house with their own hands.

"When my husband and I got married in '63 we dug the foundation by hand and built it stick by stick," Marsha says. "We added on in '66."

Their ranch home had three bedrooms, a three-car garage, four outbuildings and an in-ground pool.

"What was left of it was pulled down," Marsha says. Since then, the Callaways have been looking at property in the country, but they did not immediately find anything they liked.

Since the tornado, the couple has been living with friends, but Marsha says it is not easy.

"I have been reduced to a bedroom. What's left of my stuff is in the basement."

Marsha says she used to bake all the time. Once after the tornado she attempted to bake cookies at her friends' house.

"It took me three hours to do what I used to do in one." Marsha has not baked anything since.

**Gloria and Clarence Capps**, near Pawnee and Greenwich, were among the first people in their neighborhood to rebuild and move back to the site of their old home. Insurance covered all of their loss and more.

"We got $1,000 for car rental and we only used $185 of it because we found a car on the second day," Gloria says. "I'm using more of the money to rebuild the house, but we're not rebuilding any outbuildings, not buying a second car. We're coming out all right."

Despite rebuilding basically the same design they had before, the Capps did make one change: They built a basement.

The Capps say they have felt few lasting effects from the tornado. Although both received bruises and cuts from their experience, neither was seriously injured. However, after the tornado Gloria was not so lucky. During a fishing trip to Oklahoma to unwind, she broke her leg.

**Hartlan, Dianne Coats and their three children**, River Oaks Mobile Home Park, have found a house in the same school district. Most important, the new house has a basement.

As much as possible, Hartlan and Dianne tried to maintain life as usual for their children after the tornado. They sent them immediately back to school and quickly

The remains of Paula and Herb Bruces' home are surrounded by jagged trees. Photo by Doug Bruce.

The rebuilt Cox Farm is back in business. Photo by Trish Birk.

resumed their sports activities. The children even received support from children in California.

"There was a school in California that went through the earthquake, and those children made packets and sent them to the kids here," Hartlan says. "The packets had things like books, pictures to color, toothpaste, little homemade things in them."

**Cheryl Contreras her children, and her grandchildren,** Cottage Grove-Oaklawn, have repaired their home and moved back in.

But for a long time after the tornado, Cheryl could not make herself put things on the walls of her new home. When she finally discussed it with her counselor, they decided that she was avoiding the final step in creating a home again.

"I was afraid I would lose it all again," Cheryl says. "It was OK to get the new things, but I was also thinking, 'It could all be taken away again.'"

**The families of Cox Farm** on South Seneca had been planning to open their market for the season on April 27. After the tornado destroyed their facilities, the efforts of customers and friends allowed them to reopen their business only 30 days after the tornado.

But more than the business had been destroyed. Every one of the homes owned by the members of the family had been destroyed. Almost all of the family members lived on or near the business and worked there.

Insurance covered about two-thirds of their losses. The federal government, though FEMA, provided some money to replace the housing of one member of the family. The Small Business Administration granted a home loan to another member.

Immediately after the storm, the Salvation Army found apartments for all. Family by family, they were moving or preparing to move to their own homes.

Helen Stein and her husband, Charlie, built a new house southeast of the market. Her 90-year-old mother Daisy M. Cox lives with them. They were to move to the house exactly four months after the tornado.

Ron Stein and his family lived in an apartment in Wichita while they prepared to build a new home on the property.

Helen's sister, Violet Bishop, who also works at the market, chose to buy a home two miles away instead of across the street. Ronnie Ray Stein bought a house farther from the home property and Helen's other son Don plans to build nearby.

Together the family members give themselves the moral support needed to keep the business and their lives together.

"If one of you quits," Ron says, "you're messing with everybody's life. There's so many of us to take care of. You can't just worry about yourself. You have to worry about everybody else."

**Peggy and Clarence Gilbert**, Minnie Street, at first lived in a 15-foot travel trailer. Four months after the tornado, they moved into a double-wide modular home placed over the foundation of their old home.

Insurance paid for only part of their $68,000 loss. The Small Business Administration offered them a $30,000,

Daisy Cox moved in with her daughter Helen Stein and her husband, Charlie, after they built a new house to replace the one destroyed by the tornado. Photo by Trish Birk.

The process of rebuilding continues in two Wichita neighborhoods. A rebuilt house and a damaged house stand side by side near Pawnee and Greenwich in the photo at the left.

Right: In Sun Valley (right), newly rebuilt homes surround all that remains of one house, a stone fireplace. Photos by Carol Duerksen.

*"I never thought I would have dreams about anything that happened to me, but three and four months after the tornado, I was having some nightmares."*

–Lance Darling

30-year loan, but the elderly couple refused because of time it would take to repay the loan. Because they were eligible for the SBA loan, they could not get a grant through FEMA.

Peggy says she does not mind the loss of most of her possessions, but many losses cannot be replaced. In her old kitchen, for example, there was a special board where she had notched the heights of her grandchildren as they grew. The board flew away with the tornado.

The tornado also left the couple with an unexpected legacy. Shortly before the storm, Clarence had put 5 pounds of sunflower seeds into the bird feeder. The tornado sucked all the sunflower seeds out of the feeder and months later, sunflowers bloomed throughout their yard.

**Linda Levernez and her family**, Minnie Street, were able to move back into their damaged home almost immediately after the storm. But the first few weeks were not easy. Linda says she felt like she was moving about in a daze.

"If it wasn't for the Red Cross, the kids wouldn't have gotten fed properly like they did," she says, praising the Red Cross for bringing meals every day for weeks.

The Salvation Army also wrote vouchers to allow residents to buy needed supplies. A new spirit of community and cooperation filled the neighborhood, she says. People brought in chain saws to cut trees. Sheriff's deputies directed traffic and kept looters away.

By August, Linda and her family were making progress toward putting the tornado behind them. They had rebuilt their garage and had plans to add a tornado shelter to their home in the spring.

When the garage was done, Clarence Gilbert strolled across the street to look it over. He approved, but Linda says he added one thought:

"Next time, why don't you keep it on your side of the road?"

**Ray Macheda and Lance Darling**, near Pawnee and Greenwich, rented housing in Wichita and continued to struggle with the emotional aftermath of the storm.

"I never thought I would have dreams about anything that happened to me," Darling says, "but three and four months after the tornado, I was having some nightmares."

Macheda says, "One thing that I think is important is not to keep it inside, but to talk about it. We are both willing to talk about what we're feeling."

**Keri Montgomery, 14,** was orphaned when the tornado killed her mother, Charlene Montgomery. Two young cousins also died in the storm. All were killed while mother, cousins and Keri were attempting to get to a house with a basement. Keri suffered a broken back in the storm but was recovering. She was not paralyzed. Keri moved to Oklahoma to live with relatives. Her father died when she was 6 years old.

**Meyers Garden Spot Nursery and Greenhouse** quickly reopened, selling flowers and plants outdoors. A mobile home took the place of the office building that was destroyed.

**J.C. Pruitt,** near Pawnee and Greenwich, found

The frame is all that remains of the outside of a greenhouse at Meyer's Garden Spot Nursery and Greenhouse. Miraculously, many of the flowers inside survived. Photo by Herbert Mendenhall.

As rebuilding continues, Chris, Justin and Nick Williams (left to right) stand next to their father's 1986 Firebird. Photo by Carol Duerksen.

recovery efforts to be difficult once the initial outpouring of assistance ended.

The helping agencies like the Red Cross, Salvation Army and Mennonite Disaster Service were wonderful, he says. But despite the wealth of assistance, the family home was still unlivable many months after the tornado struck. The yard was still full of debris.

Pruitt moved his family into one of his rental houses, while his own home was repaired. But yard clean-up and the repair of the house has been progressing slowly because the family has been doing it themselves with the help of a few relatives, Pruitt says.

**Craig Reiserer,** Kellogg and 143rd, has bought a home in nearby Paul's Valley, but he says he still feels the loss of the storm.

"I lost things you can't replace, like certain antiques, pictures of every car I've owned, fraternity pictures," Reiserer says. "When you lose so much, every little thing you find in the rubble means a lot. I found my grandfather clock. It's not in perfect shape, but I'm proud to display it with it's tornado scars."

Immediately after the storm, Reiserer received help from the Mennonite Disaster Service and dozens of other friends and acquaintances.

"Until you're a victim, you don't know how much you appreciate other people's help," he says. "The Mennonites were wonderful. They came here with three

pickups full of people and in three to four hours they had made piles of wood, brick and other possessions for me to go through, then they went on to another place.

"I work a lot of hours, but I can tell you, if this happens to someone else, I'll be there to help."

Reiserer says he received 60 telephone calls at work the day after the tornado from people offering to help. He has received six or seven letters from people sending him things that fell in their yards when the items included identification and an address. Often the mailings include a note that says, "We hope you came through the storm all right."

**Lee Williams and his family,** Cottage Grove-Oaklawn, were dealing with the emotional aftermath months after the tornado passed.

Williams' 8-year-old son Justin became obsessed with the weather, Williams says. At first, that meant wanting to hear his father read from his Pilots' Ground School workbook, particularly the part about weather conditions.

"We aren't doing that anymore, but he still watches the Weather Channel real close when there's clouds in the sky," Williams says. "For a while, he would sit in the closet we all were in when the tornado hit, and he'd watch the Weather Channel from there. We've talked him out of that too, but he's still very interested in the weather." Δ

*"I work a lot of hours, but I can tell you this. If this happens to someone else, I'll be there to help."*

–Craig Reiserer

Jack and Chelsea McCreery's yard is littered with equipment. The remains of two trailers are at center. A damaged combine is top right. A building used to stand in front of the trailers. Photo by Colleen Heitman.

Right: The back wall is the only wall still standing in the McCreery's house. Photo by Colleen Heitman.

# Portrait of the Struggle

*"I had been silent during and after the storm, mainly because I felt hopeless and cheated.*

–Chelsea McCreery

"I had been silent during and after the storm, mainly because I felt hopeless and cheated." These are the words Chelsea McCreery, 49, wrote on a questionnaire she completed months after the April 26 tornado leveled the farm and smashed most of the equipment that she and her husband Jack, 53, used in their custom harvesting business. The questionnaire, which she completed for this book, was the first time Chelsea had spoken for publication about the storm. Jack had been quoted several times.

The McCreery farm near Clearwater was one of the first destroyed by the tornado that smashed thousands of homes in Haysville, Wichita and Andover and killed 17 people. Only a few hours before the tornado struck, Jack had unloaded the last of three new combines, each costing $130,000.

The couple survived the tornado by taking cover in their basement. When they climbed to the surface, Jack and Chelsea saw that the three-bedroom home they had designed themselves had been destroyed. Among the other damage was the destruction of the two mobile homes they lived in while traveling from harvesting job to harvesting job. One combine had been turned into twisted metal. The other combines were battered and heavily damaged.

In all, the damage in their farm was estimated at $750,000 – all occurring shortly before they were to set out on their annual trek through the nation, following the wheat harvest.

The night of the tornado, a trade association called U.S. Custom Harvesters Inc. put out the word that the McCreerys needed help. Almost immediatly, help began to arrive. Rick Ferris, a harvester from northwestern Kansas,

took the damaged combines 350 miles to the dealer. Harvesters in Inman and Kiowa loaned trucks. Gerald Heim of Hoxie Implement where Jack had bought the combines helped the couple negotiate with the insurance company. A motor home was loaned by a customer. Jack and Chelsea welcomed the help.

"We appreciate everyone that helped us because we couldn't have made it without your support," Chelsea writes.

But the struggle to rebuild was exhausting.

"Staying in business was our first priority and to do this we would need to go further into debt," Chelsea writes. "That was a hard thing to do at our age.

"During the summer it was difficult to do our custom harvesting because we had an astronomical amount of paper work, phone calls, and more forms to fill out. Physically the hours and pressure was tremendous. Emotionally I cried a lot. Jack was so involved in trying to stay in business, it occupied all his time. Neither of us slept much and everything seemed to upset us.

"The extra storm work has taken away from our earning power this season because we couldn't get to the fields on time due to the extra work from the storm. We had to set up different equipment, license and insure them, schedule workers, make extra trips to get equipment, spend days cleaning up and sealing the basement...We had to do this away from home sitting on a wheat job in a small town..

"We are now in the Mississippi Delta and when I think about this being our last stop, I think that I used to have a home and buildings to go home to and now the thought of going home to nothing is frightening, especially with winter fast approaching." Δ

Dirt swirls around the base of a tornado southwest of Clearwater minutes before the funnel destroys the homes of Tom and Karen Heitman and Aileen Lauterbach on May 16. Photo by June Sparr.

Right: The April 26 tornado that later ravaged Wichita and Andover appears as a white funnel towering over a neighbor's house in this photo that Cathy Chase took from her porch in Haysville.

# Myths About Tornadoes

Kansas, Texas, Oklahoma, Nebraska, parts of Missouri:

It is the roll call of Tornado Alley, the birthplace of more tornadoes than anyplace else in the world. To survive here takes heads-up alertness and an understanding of the basic rules of tornado safety.

That's the bad news. The good news is that survival is not difficult if the right precautions are taken.

To gain an understanding of the dangers, look first at the reality behind some of the myths that have grown up about tornadoes and the nation's severe weather warning system.

Taken at 6:33 p.m. on April 26, this photo is the first of a series by Mitch Abeyta showing the killer tornado as it rolls through Andover and into the countryside. Golden Spur Mobile Home Park, which was hit at 6:40 p.m., is just to the right of the funnel. Also see photos pages 110-113.

**Myth #1 — The drop in atmospheric pressure caused by a tornado is the main cause of all the damage. Therefore, it is important to open your windows when tornadoes approach.**

Reality — Most damage done by tornadoes comes from the combined action of the strong rotating winds and the impact of windborne debris, the Weather Service reports. Houses can seem to explode, but it isn't the change in pressure that is causing the house to come apart.

"In the most simple case, the force of the tornado's winds push the windward wall of a building inward," according to *Tornado Safety*, a Weather Service publication. "The roof is lifted up and the other walls fall outward."

This means that opening a window generally will do little to minimize damage. In fact, opening the wrong window can increase the damage.

**Myth #2 — You can always spot a tornado because all tornadoes look alike.**

Reality — Although most tornadoes appear as some version of the classic funnel shape, they can also look far different. The funnel shape may be absent in particularly large and powerful tornadoes, the most dangerous tornadoes of all.

"The tornado may appear to be a large, turbulent cloud near the ground," according to *Tornado Safety*. "It may even be mistaken for a large rain shaft or even a non-weather event such as a fire."

Several people in Andover and Wichita reported that the tornado looked like a huge turbulent cloud or a dark wall that was moving toward them.

Tornadoes can also appear as long thin ropes that are almost parallel to the ground. Although this usually happens late in a tornado's life when it has shrunk in size, such a twister can still be very dangerous. A

A funnel forms near Charles Brewer's field southeast of Potwin on May 26. "So many parts are rotating in this cloud." Brewer says. "The big main part is putting down tails and then they go back up." Photo by Charles Brewer.

**Right:** A July 1991 thunderstorm discharges fingers of lightning in Wichita. Photo by Audie Thornburg.

At 6:36 p.m. on April 26, the tornado nears the Golden Spur Mobile Home Park. Photographer Mitch Abeyta and photographer Richard Parks, whose mother lived in Golden Spur, took dozens of photos as they watched the tornado from east of Andover. Photo by Mitch Abeyta.

twister's color can also vary. In the 1991 Kansas twisters, people reported seeing various shades of white, brown and black.

### Myth #3 — Tornadoes can always be located by their characteristic sound.

Reality — Although tornadoes often produce a rumbling or roaring sound similar to that of a train or airplane, sound is not always a clue to the approach of a tornado. Many people have reported seeing a tornado before hearing it. Others reported that they never heard any kind of roar, even when the tornado was directly overhead.

However, at night or during a heavy rain, a rumble or roar may be the only evidence of a tornado's presence, the Weather Service says.

"Thunderstorms can also produce violent straight-line winds which produce a similar sound," according to *Tornado Safety*. "If any unusual roar is heard during threatening weather, it is best to take cover immediately."

### Myth #4 — Only one tornado appears at a time. It is always safe to relax after a tornado has swept through your area.

Reality — Two or more tornadoes can be associated with a single thunderstorm. At times, several tornadoes can occur at the same moment, extending downward from the same thunderstorm, according to *Tornado Safety*.

"As the parent thunderstorm moves along, tornadoes may form, travel along in contact with the ground, and

dissipate or lift, followed shortly by other tornado touchdowns, and so on," the booklet says. "Tornadoes can also be made up of a number of smaller but intense vortices that rotate about a common center. With this type, the most intense damage is concentrated along the paths of the small vortices."

Tornadoes can also occur in clusters. On April 26, as many as 20 twisters may have touched down in Kansas. The largest tornado outbreak in history occurred on April 3 and 4, 1974 when 178 tornadoes swept across 13 states, including Kentucky, Tennessee, Ohio and Indiana. The tornadoes killed more than 300 people, injured more than 6,000 and caused $600 million in damage.

### Myth #5 — You can outrun a tornado in a car.

Reality — Many people have died trying to do this. On average, tornadoes travel at a speed of 30 miles per hour, but speeds as high as 70 miles per hour have been reported. Tornadoes can also take erratic paths and change direction suddenly, even though most tornadoes move from the southwest to the northeast.

"In populated areas, it is very dangerous to attempt to flee to safety in an automobile," according to *Tornado Safety*. "Over half of the deaths in the Wichita Falls (Texas) tornado of 1979 were attributed to people trying to escape in motor vehicles. While chances of avoiding a tornado by driving away in a vehicle may be better in open country, it is still best in most cases to seek or remain in a sturdy shelter such as a house or building. Even a ditch or ravine offers better protection than a vehicle."

The April 26 tornado is framed by two trees as it moves through Haysville in this photo taken by Greg Mullins from his house in south Wichita.

Right: Taken from 71st and Meridian looking northeast, this photo shows the April 26 tornado as it grinds through Haysville. Photo by John Coleman.

**Myth #6 — All tornadoes occur in the afternoon and early evening. Don't worry about tornadoes any other time during the day.**

Reality — Although most tornadoes occur between 3 p.m. to 7 p.m., they can occur at any time. Often they occur with little or no warning.

**Myth #7 — Mobile homes provide safe shelter during a tornado, particularly if the mobile home is firmly anchored to the ground.**

Reality — Mobile homes do not provide adequate shelter under any circumstances, says Fred Ostby, director of the National Severe Storms Forecast Center in Kansas City.

In the April 26 tornado that ravaged Sedgwick and Butler counties, for example, 11 of the 17 people who died were in or near the Golden Spur Mobile Home Park in Andover. In contrast, no one died in a development of constructed homes that was destroyed directly across the street from Golden Spur. The rest of the deaths in Wichita and Andover were among people who were caught outside when the storm struck. Both people who died in Cowley and Elk counties on April 26 were also in mobile homes.

Mobile homes are particularly vulnerable to tornadoes because they are relatively light structures with broad sides, according to *Tornado Safety*. Mobile homes can easily by overturned by winds.

"Their thin walls make them extremely vulnerable to wind-blown debris," the publication warns. "Even if tied down, they should be evacuated for more substantial shelter. Mobile home parks should have storm shelters

for their residents if located in areas where strong thunderstorms or tornadoes occur."

On April 26, more than 200 residents of Golden Spur took shelter in the park's storm cellar. All of them survived.

It is particularly important for residents in mobile homes to go to appropriate shelter when a tornado warning is issued, Ostby says. Don't wait to check out the weather yourself. Don't wait for anything.

**Myth #8 — Outdoor sirens, controlled by local officials, are the most important part of the tornado warning system. It is always safe to wait to take cover until you hear a siren.**

Reality — It is never safe to wait for sirens. Sirens may fail to work as they did in Andover. Since no law requires local governments to purchase and run sirens, the warning system may not even be used in your area. If you live in a rural area, you may be too far away from sirens to hear the warning.

In reality, sirens are not supposed to be the final warning to take cover, Ostby says. The sirens' role is to warn people who are outdoors and may not have heard warnings issued on radio and television.

The best warning system for any individual is a combination of personal alertness and radio or television, which can tell when a tornado has been sighted on the ground. Listen for tornado watches or severe thunderstorm watches, which are issued by the Weather Service when conditions are right to produce tornadoes or severe thunderstorms.

Remember that any thunderstorm can produce a

At 6:39 p.m,, April 26, the tornado destroys much of Andover. Photo by Mitch Abeyta.

A wall cloud looms over Lincoln County on April 12. The rotation within the cloud is visible at the center of the photo. A tornado later dropped out of the cloud near Sylvan Grove. Photo by Russel Parsons.

**Right:** This March 26 tornado struck Brad and Penny Wilt's house, near Abbyville a few minutes after this photo was taken. Brad and Penny were standing inside their back door looking southwest when Penny snapped the picture.

At 6:40 p.m., April 26, the tornado hits the Golden Spur Mobile Home Park. Photo by Mitch Abeyta.

tornado. When a watch has been issued, listen and watch for tornadoes and take cover if conditions seem threatening. Small tornadoes can strike before warnings can be issued, meteorologists say.

For the best access to weather information, buy what the weather service calls a NOAA Weather Radio. NOAA stands for the National Oceanic and Atmospheric Administration. The radio can be tuned to a broadcast station run by the local officials of the Weather Service. Each station gives a constant stream of information about the weather.

The radio also comes with an alarm that can wake you when weather watches or warnings are issued at night. When a watch or warning is issued in your area by the Weather Service, the radio emits a tone that sounds a bit like a high-pitched electronic alarm clock. The radio then turns itself on to provide the latest information about the weather.

The radios usually sell for about $40 at electronics stores such as Radio Shack. Δ

# The Key to Survival

The Weather Service advises that the "key to survival" is planning.

"All members of a household should know where the safest areas of home are," according to *Tornado Safety*. "Identify interior bathrooms, closets, halls, or basement shelter areas. Be sure every family member knows that they should move to such safe areas at the first signs of danger. There may be only seconds to act."

Every workplace should have a tornado emergency plan. Schools should form a plan and conduct drills, the Weather Service says.

Most injuries and deaths in tornadoes are caused by flying debris. That is why small rooms like closets or bathrooms in the center of a building offer the best shelter, the weather service says. Always avoid windows, which can shatter, or exterior doors, which can blow open or even blow away.

"Storm cellars or well-constructed basements offer the greatest protection from tornadoes," according to the booklet. "If neither is available, the lowest floor of any substantial structure offers the best alternative. In high-rise buildings, it may not be practical for everyone to reach the lower floors, but the occupants should move as far down as possible and take shelter in interior, small rooms or stairwells."Δ

A tornado rolls through Washington Couty on April 26. Photo by Investigator Delbert Hawel.

Right: Lightning strikes from a thunderstorm 1 mile south of Mulvane. Photo by Don Blecha

# The Weather Service Warning System

**Thunderstorm or Tornado Watch** — A watch is issued when the weather service determines that thunderstorms and/or tornadoes are **most likely to occur.**

* Severe Thunderstorm Watch — This means that thunderstorms in the area may produce large and damaging hail and/or damaging winds. This also means that tornadoes may occur. Every severe thunderstorm has the potential to spawn tornadoes.

* Tornado Watch — Conditions are favorable for both tornadoes and severe thunderstorms. During a tornado watch everyone in or near the watch area should watch for signs of dangerous weather, listen to NOAA Weather Radio or commercial radio or television. Make preliminary plans to seek shelter.

**Severe Thunderstorm or Tornado Warning** — Warnings are issued when severe thunderstorms or tornadoes have been indicated by radar or reported by trained spotters or other credible sources like police officers. A warning describes the area at risk. The Weather Service suggests listening closely to the information contained in the warning. If a tornado has been sighted nearby, take shelter immediately.

"At times, you may be in a warning area, but the reported tornado may not be nearby," according to *Tornado Safety*. "Remember, you may still be at risk and should be prepared to take cover since the storm may be moving your way or may even produce additional tornadoes or damaging winds."

People in mobile homes should go immediately to the basement of a nearby friend or a shelter in the mobile home park. Δ

At 6:42 p.m., April 26, the killer tornado was only two miles from photographer Mitch Abeyta. This is the closest the funnel came to Abeyta.

# Fatal Kansas Tornadoes

May 30, 1879 — Irving; 66 dead.

May 17, 1896 — Brown and Washington counties; 25 dead.

May 5, 1905 — Ellsworth and McPherson counties; 29 dead.

May 25, 1917 — Sedgwick and Marion counties; 23 dead.

Nov. 11, 1917 — Great Bend; 11 dead.

May 25, 1955 — Udall; 80 dead.

June 10, 1958 — El Dorado; 15 dead.

June 8, 1966 — Topeka; 12 dead.

June 8, 1974 — Emporia, 6 dead.

# In Honor of 20 Kansans

The tornadoes of April 26 killed 20 Kansans. Nineteen died in Kansas, and one died heading toward home on an Oklahoma highway. But the statistics cannot begin to tell their story. Seconds before the tornadoes struck, each had been a vital human being. Each had their dreams. Each was loved by someone else. Here is a brief look at their lives and deaths.

### Mathilda Bebout, 67.

Although Mathilda Bebout retired from teaching three years ago, she had not slowed down.

Active in her church, the First Church of the Nazarene, working a part-time job with a doctor, volunteering at Botonica gardens and participating in the Kennel Club kept her busy.

An enthusiastic instructor, Ms. Bebout was one of the original teachers at Booth Elementary School in Wichita.

She loved her three dogs dearly and may have been trying to bring one of them into her home near Pawnee and Greenwich when she was killed.

### Joe Bobbitt, 66.

Easy to laugh, Joe Bobbitt was a man at ease with himself and others.

"You could sit and talk to him and laugh," says a friend, Mary Lou Spencer.

A lifelong cowboy, Mr. Bobbitt always worked for horse people.

A year before the tornado, both Mr. Bobbitt and his friend Ruby Crawford played a vital role when they helped Spencer survive the death of her husband Chuck.

"If I needed anything, they were there to help me," Spencer says.

No one knows where Mr. Bobbitt was when the tornado struck. The home he shared with Ms. Crawford was destroyed. Mr. Bobbitt was found among the debris of the park. His chest had been crushed.

### Susan Elizabeth Cravens, 2
### Anna Marie Cravens, 5.

The girls were the joy of lives of Leonard and Kathleen Cravens of Wichita.

"We'd always made it a priority to be with the girls," Leonard says. "We would work our job schedules out so one of us could be with them, rather than taking them to a babysitter. It was important for us to be with them in their growing up years."

On the night of the tornado, the Cravens were treating themselves to a rare restaurant dinner while the girls visited their aunt, Charlene Montgomery, and their cousin, Keri. The girls and their aunt died near Pawnee and Greenwich in Wichita as the four of them struggled to reach the shelter of a neighbor's basement. Keri was seriously injured.

### Ruby Crawford, 58.

Ruby Crawford died as she had lived, Mary Lou Spencer says. Ms. Crawford died trying to help others. In fact, Ms. Crawford died while trying to help Mary Lou's frail, elderly parents, Gladys and Robert Manes, reach the Golden Spur tornado shelter.

Known as the Golden Spur's unofficial grandmother, Ms. Crawford was the manager of the Andover Senior Citizens Center. If people needed help they went to her. Often she didn't even wait for a cry for help, but approached others first.

"Ruby enjoyed taking care of people," Mary Lou says. Ms. Crawford and her friend, Joe Bobbitt, also enjoyed the simple pleasure of an afternoon with friends.

"I'd go and sit by the hour and talk," Mary Lou says. "They knew my kids, and I knew their kids. We'd just visit. That they really loved."

### G.D. "Dale" Davis, 57.

G.D. "Dale" Davis, a Wichita businessman, died on April 26 when a tornado swept his car off the Cimarron Turnpike in Oklahoma.

Ron Smith, an accountant who worked for Davis, was also in the car and was seriously injured.

A native of Pawnee, Ok., Davis died not far from where he was born. He graduated in 1955 from what is now called Oklahoma State University and four years later started his own oil well logging company.

Now called Davis Great Guns Logging, the company is one of two that were owned by Davis. The other company, known as Digital Logging, manufactures logging equipment in Tulsa.

Mr. Davis and Smith apparently pulled off the road when they saw the storm coming, but they could find no place to hide. They tried to ride out the storm by sitting in their car with their seatbelts on, but the tornado picked up the car.

### Marilyn Decker, 29.

A certified nurse's aide at Winfield State Hospital, Marilyn Decker was passionate about her work with mentally retarded patients.

She lived in Wellington near Wichita before moving to Cowley County 18 months before the tornado. She died when the funnel struck her mobile home.

### Lucille Jacobs, 79.

Lucille Jacobs was known as a quiet woman who loved to crochet and knit, and she excelled at her hobbies.

She loved reading the Bible and crocheting afghans for her 21 grandchildren and 15 great-grandchildren.

Ms. Jacobs and her husband were in their mobile home when the tornado struck. Her husband survived.

### Ronald Kanavy I, 47
### Ronald Kanavy II, 23

The father and son died when they took shelter in a ditch near Golden Spur. The two men and their wife and mother, Pat Kanavy, had been driving to visit friends when they encountered the tornado.

The senior Mr. Kanavy owned a fix-it shop and worked as a welder and fabricator at Central Steel in Wichita. The son worked as a cashier at Coastal Mart while he studied to become an auto mechanic.

The summer of 1991 would have marked the 27th wedding anniversary for Pat and Ronald Kanavy I.

When the tornado hit, both men shielded Pat with their bodies by lying on top of her in the ditch.

### Elsie Kemper, 58.

Elsie Kemper was known around Golden Spur for cultivating one of the prettiest flower gardens in the park.

She worked at Wichita Industries and Services for the Blind. Recently Ms. Kemper was given an award by her employer for coming up with a way to save money by recycling scrap paper.

Mrs. Kemper died after she and her husband Anton had dashed to a metal shed to take shelter from the tornado. Her husband survived.

### Gladys Manes, 85
### Robert Manes, 89.

Gladys and Robert Manes were looking forward to a Memorial Day outing on a daughter's pontoon boat.

Although age and illness had recently begun to take a toll on the couple, the two were known throughout their lives for their energy and their interest in the outdoors. They often took all nine grandchildren camping, including trips to Yosemite National Park.

For years the two had farmed 160 acres of wheat, corn and oats in Iowa. In the last few years, the work had gotten to be too difficult. Finally, the two were unable to care for themselves. Relatives moved the couple to the Wichita and Andover area, says their daughter, Mary Lou Spencer. On the day of the tornado, the Manes were staying with Mary Lou in her mobile home in Golden Spur.

"We brought them down here so they would be safe," Spencer says.

Liz Spencer, Mary Lou's daughter-in-law, describes Robert Manes as a strong man.

"He was a big strong farmer," she says. "He had strong values and you didn't cross him...

"Grandma, she had a unique way of knowing when you needed an enouraging letter. Whenever (my husband) Roger and I would be having any kind of problem, financial or something going on we were having trouble handling, we got a letter, usually a poem. She would cut out articles she found and send them to you or verses from the Bible."

The Maneses died before they could reach the Golden Spur's tornado shelter.

### Joe Marks, 68.

Joe Marks was well known in Golden Spur — and Livingston's Restaurant.

Mr. Marks was gruff and independent and rarely cooked a meal for himself. Often he would eat at Livingston's. When waitresses asked him what he wanted to eat, he would often reply, "How should I know!"

He enjoyed sitting on his porch, even during tornado

warnings. On the night of the tornado, Mr. Marks stayed true to his habit of ignoring the alerts. He refused to go to the shelter.

Mr. Marks was retired from the International Cold Storage Co. He never talked about what he had done in his working life, neighbor Jim Fairman says.

Neighbors said he loved his three dogs. Mr. Marks has a sister in Illinois.

### Robert Meininger, 46.

Fun-loving and outgoing, Robert Meininger was a craftsman who worked as a glazier for Lewis Street Glass in Wichita and loved working with his hands.

"He enjoyed his job immensely, even did some work after hours," says his daughter, Teresa Warren. "He loved building and making things."

Mr. Meininger made a replica out of glass of the building where he worked.

For years, Mr. Meininger and Teresa had not been close. He had been divorced from her mother when she was 13. But recently father and daughter had gotten together.

"We had built an extremely good relationship," Warren says. "My dad was my friend as well as my father. I could tell my father anything."

Mr. Meininger had lived in the Golden Spur Mobile Home Park in Andover since 1979. He died when he left the park shelter and went back to lock his house.

### Charlene Montgomery, 47.

A group leader at Beech Aircraft Co. in Wichita, Ms. Montgomery had raised her children alone since her husband died eight years ago.

Keri, 14, still lived at home. An older daughter, Terri Kastner, had married a soldier.

Until a few weeks before the tornado, Terri had been living at home while her husband served in Saudi Arabia. When her husband was transferred back to Fort Benning, Ga., Terri went back to Georgia to be with him.

### Denise Peterson, 28.

The last six months of Denise Peterson's life were probably her happiest.

A veterinary clinic technician, Ms. Peterson had finally gotten her independence by buying a mobile home in Golden Spur. She was doing a job "she absolutely adored," says her mother Geraldine Peterson of Derby.

Although she earned a degree in history from Kansas State University, Ms. Peterson's love of animals led her to study veterinary science at Colby Community College. She was working with an Andover veterinarian at the time of her death.

Energetic, Ms. Peterson racked up several miles running a day. She also rode a bike and walked. She was 4 foot 9. A few weeks before the tornado she reached her weight goal of 92 pounds.

After she died, her family received a Visa bill and discovered that she had just bought $300 worth of new clothes to celebrate.

"At least she got to enjoy shopping for them," her mother says. Ms. Peterson liked to watch pro wrestling on TV and she loved old movies, especially the Wizard of Oz. Interested in the movie since childhood, Ms. Peterson read up on Judy Garland and became something of an authority on the actress.

Her mother reports that the family has received many letters from friends since the tornado.

"We received notes from everywhere telling how much she changed lives. Some were pages long."

A scholarship fund has been established in Ms. Peterson's name at the junior college. Ms. Peterson died in Golden Spur.

## Betty Sanders, 61.

Betty Sanders was a bit famous around Golden Spur. Known for her friendly nature, Ms. Sanders was equally famous for her "pickle parties." The parties featured pickles, chips and story telling.

Ms. Sanders and her husband Cecil were also well-known for their weekly potlucks and summer cookouts.

Ms. Sanders died in Golden Spur. Cecil Sanders had gone bowling and was not home at the time of the tornado.

## Katherine Sargent, 41.

For Katherine Sargent, the days before the tornado were happy ones. Nine months before, she had been married to Allen Sargent. She had recently celebrated the birth of a grandson.

"I couldn't have been any happier," Allen says. The two met one year and 10 days before the tornado struck. They came together at a church group called Previously Married Catholics on April 16, 1990. On July 28, 1990, they were married.

Allen is a structural draftsman at Boeing Aircraft Co. Ms. Sargent worked at City Bank at Harry and Oliver for about a year.

Allen, Ms. Sargent and two of their children were together in the Sargents' mobile home in Golden Spur when the tornado struck. Although the other family members were injured, all survived.

## Bessie Temple, 82.

On the day she died, Bessie Temple was celebrating good news from her doctor.

The retired businesswoman had just been told that she was recovering well from a heart ailment that had troubled her the year before. To celebrate the news, Ms. Temple and her sister went shopping, according to newspaper accounts.

Ms. Temple and her husband had owned several businesses, including the R&B Bait Shop at Toronto Lake. But even in retirement, she was so energetic that at age 72 she had climbed to the roof of a friend's barn to repair shingles that had been blown off by a storm.

Ms. Temple was apparently in her living room in her mobile home in Golden Spur when the storm arrived. Although she was found alive, Temple died later that evening.

She had no children. Ms. Temple had lived in Sedan for years and had recently moved to Andover to be closer to her family. ∆